One Hamlet
and
One Farm

each
Representative of Thousands

By Robert W. Bitz

LCCN: 2012915769
ISBN: 978-0-9859504-2-2
First edition, published 2012.

Ward Bitz Publishing
Baldwinsville, NY

The author may be contacted at:
P.O. Box 302
Plainville, NY 13137

Preface

W hy write about Plainville and the nearby farm where I grew up? Both are insignificant to all but a few people living today.

I write about them because they have been a significant part of my life for over 80 years and bring back many fond memories. There are deeper reasons for writing about them, however, and only with the passage of time, probably many years, will there be evidence to reveal vindication or futility.

During my lifetime, especially after 60 years of living, hundreds of questions have come to my mind regarding life and the happenings on our farm and in the Plainville community during the centuries before my appearance on earth. I am most appreciative of the pieces of information I have unearthed in the few books that mention some of Plainville's history. There is little history about the farm other than some Census reports and a few early 20th century photographs.

Knowledge also comes to me from other northeastern communities and farms where pieces of historical information have been recorded that fairly closely parallel what transpired in the community of Plainville and the farm where I have lived and worked. Although this history is not specific it provides a likeness, although slightly blurry.

I have seen dramatic changes in Plainville. Almost every resident's life was closely associated with the community. It was where they worked, bought their groceries, went to school and enjoyed social activities. Attractions from outside the community pulled on the residents as the automobile and improved roads appeared in the 1920s. However, the school, church, general store and fire department continued to be stronger magnets holding residents together in a cohesive community.

As additional opportunities for work, shopping, recreation and religious activities became readily available outside the community, and when the school closed there was little left to hold the community together. Plainville was gradually becoming a bedroom community, a situation that has been repeated in hundreds of communities throughout New York.

I come from farming families who have lived in rural communities, dating back multiple generations, to Germany and England of centuries ago. They came to the colonies and later to the United States to better their lives. They prospered, not excessively but with a better life, like millions of others who arrived with hopes for prosperity.

Living on farms, it is likely none of my ancestors starved but worked hard to achieve a good life. I remember how careful our family was with money. There had to be enough to pay the taxes, survive a drought and have enough money to live through a year when prices for farm products barely met expenses.

I was fortunate to be born in 1930. We were still in the age of horses, hand labor and difficult times. Each year the farm became slightly more mechanized and there was a gradual movement toward greater prosperity as we moved out of the Great Depression. Farming still consisted of hard physical work and long hours but new machinery removed some of the more difficult work and provided increased free time.

The 1940s and 1950s were a time in farming's history when a decision had to be made to 'get in' or 'get out'. Many farmers made the wise choice to 'get out' and prospered while others expanded their operations. Fortunately my father and I decided to 'get in' and were able to prosper, but perhaps that might not have happened during a different period of time.

The stories and pictures that follow will provide a slice of the history of the Plainville community and an insight into life on a farm during a period of dramatic change taking place throughout the world, specifically pointed at one small community and one farm. Whoever may explore these pages in the future beware. History repeats itself, not in the same exact image but in corresponding ways.

About the Author

Bob Bitz's 'roots' run deep in Plainville and in the 72 acre farm purchased by his great-great grandfather in 1835. He has lived in the 1835 home, constructed by his ancestors, for the past 59 years and previously lived in the home built by his grandfather in 1883.

Generations of Bob's ancestors, from several branches of his family, have been laid to rest in the Plainville Rural Cemetery, which sits peacefully behind the Plainville Christian Church. The three Plainville schools; first a log cabin, next a brick three-room school and last a wooden two-room school, attended by generations of his family, have all disappeared.

The family's home farm gradually increased in size from the original 72 acres to well over 1,000 acres. The team of oxen that originally pulled the walking plow evolved into tractors of several hundred horsepower that pulled behemoth plows and other equipment. The few hundred bushels of wheat and homemade butter, originally produced to purchase the farm, contrast to millions of turkeys sold throughout the country during the early 21st century.

Bob went to the Plainville school for eight years, then to Baldwinsville Academy and on to Cornell University before returning to the farm. He chose to specialize in turkey production and marketing, which had been a portion of the farm's business since 1923. Bob led the farm's operations for over 30 years before gradually turning leadership over to his son Mark in the early 90s.

While operating the farm Bob was involved in numerous local organizations, visited all 50 states, including museums in many of the states, and numerous countries scattered around the world. He strongly believes that anyone fortunate enough to have 'roots' is blessed, and that they help provide a deeper sense of being.

Bob has written several books including *A History of Agriculture in Onondaga County, Four Hundred Years of Agricultural Change in the Empire State, A History of Manufacturing in Baldwinsville and the Towns of Lysander and Van Buren, Transportation in Central New York and the Baldwinsville Area 1600 to 1940* and *Tales of a Turkey Farmer.*

At one time he had a museum on his farm entitled The Pioneer Experience and is a past director and president of the Witter Agricultural Museum. Recently he received a medal from the Onondaga Historical Association for his contributions to the history of Onondaga County.

Table of Contents

Hamlet

My Little "Big Apple"

Screaming sirens, honking horns, street walkers, masses of people and fancy restaurants were all beyond the most vivid imagination of any youngster in our local 'Big Apple' of Plainville. Calling our little crossroads community anything more than a hamlet was really a stretch of imagination. During my childhood it boasted a church, a two room school, general store, blacksmith shop, fire department and about 20 homes. A brief description of how Plainville came into existence parallels the story of the birth of hundreds of other hamlets and small villages in New York.

The glaciers passing through the northeastern part of North America were responsible for the location of Plainville. Since the purpose of roads is to move people and their goods easily from one point to another, roads in a developing community, follow the paths of least resistance, going around bodies of water and avoiding hills. Cross Lake, a nine mile long lake, with the Seneca River flowing across its southern end and then winding through the countryside largely determined Plainville's location.

When Plainville's first settlers arrived in the early 1800s, they came by oxcart, horseback or on foot. The roads were paths through the forest that could not have been navigated by wagons, if there had been any wagons. Some settlers used the Seneca River as a highway and then traveled the last few miles on foot over land. The first settlers to arrive in Plainville were the William Wilson family who came from Vermont about 1800. They settled on one of the corners of the four-corners and the hamlet was known as Wilson's Corners until it had its first post office in 1821. Until then, any mail coming to the Plainville area settlers was left in a hollow tree. Anyone passing by would pick up mail for themselves or a nearby neighbor.

Because the community requested the name Farmersville, when it applied for a post office, ironically it ended up named Plainville, probably an even more appropriate name. Since some lucky community in New York had previously chosen Farmersville as its name, the US Postal Service reached into its sack of unused names and pulled out Plainville.

In the 1790s, New York State negotiated with the Native Americans for the purchase of a huge tract of land encompassing nearly two million acres, to pay some of New York's soldiers in the Revolutionary War. The Plainville area was a tiny portion of this tract. Very few Revolutionary veterans settled on the land they were granted, instead selling it to whoever would pay them a little something. As a result, this tract eventually evolved into thousands of farms and hundreds of small communities. Settlers poured into these new lands by the thousands, clearing the forests, preparing the land for crops and establishing a new life.

Every few miles, where two of these early trails crossed, a small hamlet similar to Plainville appeared to provide the services needed by those mostly self-sufficient settlers. Where there was a stream available for waterpower, additional businesses such as sawmills and gristmills appeared. Plainville, lacking any additional feature beyond the intersection of two trails, offered only the basic services of general store, hotel, school, blacksmith, church and a few small businesses like shoemaker, basket maker and wagon shop.

During the succeeding century, until I was a young boy, there were only minor changes. Small businesses came and went, roads were improved, the automobile came into use, new generations were born as the older generations passed on and Plainville remained, little changed with the passage of time.

I was born near the end of an era with relatively little progress as compared to the rapidly changing world of today. Yes, the automobile was beginning to change Plainville with the advent of the Ford

Model-T, but slowly. Those that had a car by 1920 put it up on blocks during the winter and hitched their horse to a cutter for transportation. Some people continued to use the horse for transportation into the 1930s. Money was scarce in the community and people still worked and shopped locally. Cracks were beginning to show in the fabric of the community but there was little evidence of the changes that were about to come.

I mention elsewhere in this book that the church, school and general store were the glue that held the community together. The automobile was the force that gradually melted the glue. Before the automobile arrived, the only way to travel from Plainville was by walking or with a horse. A stagecoach passed through Plainville, but only once a day, requiring an overnight stay if you traveled more than a few miles. The dirt roads through Plainville were replaced with concrete in the early 1920s permitting much faster travel and opening up job opportunities 20 miles away. People working away from the community found improved shopping opportunities, a wider circle of friends and a variety of churches to satisfy their needs. Gradually the general store lost customers and membership in the local church decreased. Improved roads and buses made it easy for children to be transported to schools in larger communities that were considered to offer improved education. With the closing of the Plainville School in the 1960s, the glue that held the community together had almost totally disappeared. Plainville had become a bedroom community for its residents with school, church, shopping and friends scattered in all directions.

Life is always changing around us, but normally so slowly that we don't realize what is happening. Even though the speed of change in the middle 1900s was much more rapid than during the previous 100 years, few of us realized the ramifications and the extent of the change. My little 'Big Apple' gradually disintegrated in front of my eyes and moved slowly; first to nearby Baldwinsville, then the city of Syracuse, later to New York City, but now my 'Big Apple' encompasses the entire world! Yes, Plainville certainly has changed but along with its change I have changed, even more.

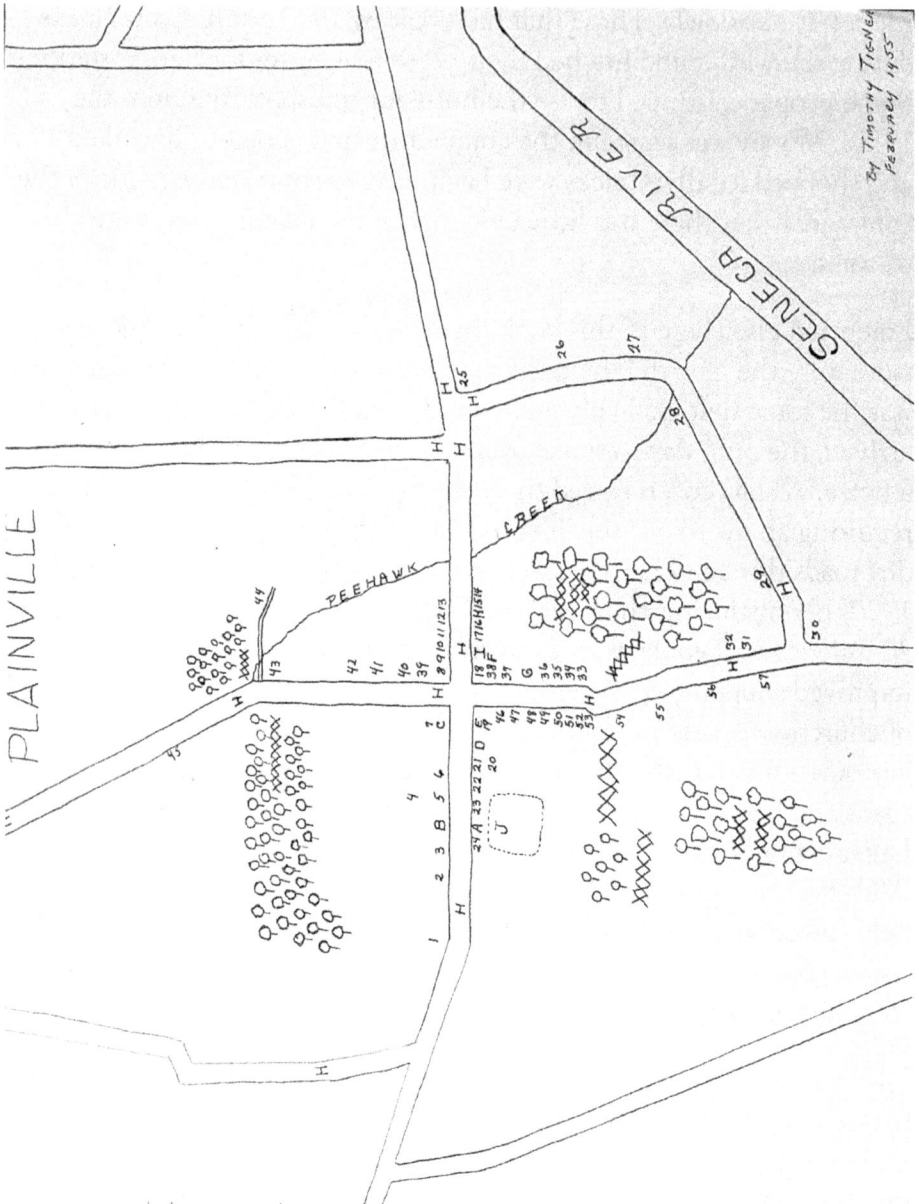

A 1958 aerial photograph of Plainville. Church parsonage, barn, church and cemetery are in the right foreground. The school and its playground are in the left foreground. The general store is on the left at the four-corners and the blacksmith shop is kitty-corner from the store on the four-corners. The firehouse is just behind the blacksmith shop. The hall is the tall building with the white roof about five buildings to the right of the blacksmith shop. Courtesy of Marilyn Hollenbeck

(left) A map of Plainville drawn in 1955 by Timothy Tigner, a school student and son of Reverend Hugh and Julia Tigner. Tim numbered the homes and provided the last names of the residents at that time. He provides letters to mark the public buildings.

A photograph of the Plainville Christian Church taken in 2012. This building was constructed in 1854, two years after the wooden church, located slightly to the east, burned.

Plainville Christian Church

Simple yet elegant, the church in Plainville sat on the top of a gentle hill with its tall steeple visible from all directions, beckoning one and all. Constructed of brick in 1854, after the previous wooden church had been destroyed by fire in 1852, it has welcomed generations of newborn babies and said goodbye, lifetimes later. It was a non-denominational church founded in a log building, constructed in May 1822, which also served as a school. Church services continued in the log building until a new church was constructed in 1831.

Until the 1940s, the church, the school and the general store were the glue that held the community together. Local residents either went to church or not; it wasn't a case of where, since other churches in neighboring villages were considered too far away. The area cemetery was located directly behind the church. There, each one who had lived in the community rested in its shadow. On Memorial Day all who were buried were remembered with ceremonies and music.

The church, on the inside as on the outside, was simple and plain but possessed a natural beauty. There were two rows of oak pews with comfortable seat cushions to ease the burden of a long service, and three large rectangular stained glass windows on each side to permit the light of the outside world to mingle with the inner beauty of the church. There was a balcony in the back of the church, to accommodate the unusual overflow congregation. This was separated into three sections for children's Sunday School classes. Sunday School classes for older children and adults were held in the four corners of the sanctuary.

Across the front of the church was a low elevated stage for the small pump organ, the choir and the minister. This was the stage where I was required, unhappily, to recite pieces for Children's Day, Christmas Exercises and other unfortunate times. There was a crude basement under the church, which housed the wood burning furnace with its huge grate above, in the center of the church aisle, bringing warmth to the congregation on cold Sunday mornings. A toilet stood in a dark, dingy corner of the basement for emergency use but was avoided if possible.

Each Sunday morning, a bell, in the belfry of the tall church steeple, sent rich tones across the countryside as it beckoned to all within hearing distance. It rang first about a half-hour before the service and the second time to call any lingering souls to its doors.

To the west of the church, about 100 feet away, was a barn that was once used as a hitching barn, for parishioners who came further than walking distance, to tie their horses. The need to travel to church with horse and buggy ended in the 1930s and the barn was used to store the necessary firewood for both the church and the home of the minister who lived next door in a house furnished by the church, called the parsonage.

During the entire life of the church, even continuing today, there has always been a shortage of money to take care of the needs of the church. As a result, church members have always been innovative in raising money and cutting costs whenever they could. A few ways the church raised money are mentioned in a chapter titled 'The Hall'. An example of the way members saved money in obtaining fuel to heat the church and the parsonage is in the next paragraph.

Each year one of the area farmers gave the needed wood from his farm's woodlot, providing the church members cut the wood and hauled it away. An appropriate winter's day was chosen and about a dozen farmers headed to the woods with crosscut saws, axes and bob sleighs, pulled by sturdy teams of horses. Some of the men started felling trees, others cut the wood into manageable lengths while others loaded the wood on the bob sleighs to be hauled and stacked near the highway. Later, on a mild winter's day, several men gathered again to buzz the wood into shorter lengths to fit appropriately into furnace and stove. One of the men had a Model-T Ford. He jacked up a rear wheel and ran a flat endless belt from the wheel to power the buzz saw. Later the wood was stored in the adjacent old hitching barn for use during the following winter. The old hitching barn has been torn down. The church's need for fuel was filled and the men enjoyed working together to supply this need.

The parishioners attitude of 'do-it-yourself' to save money extended to all repairs and maintenance for the church and parsonage. If a repair was needed, someone volunteered to perform the repair without cost. Usually there was a person capable of performing the task well.

In 1960, members of the church showed their cooperative and 'can do' nature again when they constructed a new Christian Education and Social Activity building, attached to the west side of the church. Most of the work in the construction of the building was performed by the church members, including nailing and glueing the rafters together on the floor of Charles Woods barn, near Cross Lake.

The Plainville Christian Church has served the little rural community for almost 200 years. Many challenges have been overcome and it continues doing its best to meet the community's needs. My years in the church during the 1930s and 40s bring back wonderful memories of dozens of people giving both time and money toward the betterment of the church and community.

A 1920 photograph of the back of the Plainville Christian Church following a violent wind storm. Courtesy of Marilyn Hollenbeck

The Hall

The 'Hall' served as the social center for the community church. It was a plain two-story wooden building, about twenty-four by fifty feet, built around 1900 by the AOUW (Ancient Order of United Workmen). It was used by the Grange and later owned by the Charter Oak Lodge. During the early 1900s, before automobiles and television, people in the small community came together for fellowship and entertainment. With difficult financial times and the more common use of the automobile, membership in the Lodge waned and the building was donated to the church in the early 1930s. Since the meeting place of the Charter Oak Lodge was the Charter Lodge Hall, the name was shortened and everyone called it the 'Hall'.

Rural churches never seemed to have enough money to meet their meager expenses so the Plainville Church used the Hall for a variety of money raising activities, usually associated with food. Since the Hall was also used for the local polling place, the church women decided to serve an election day chicken dinner at noon to raise money for the church and in the evening serve a chicken, biscuit and gravy supper to use up the leftover chicken.

The voting area and the kitchen were both downstairs with the dining room upstairs. There was a single flight of stairs leading to the upper level, used by both diners and for the transport of food, as well as for removal of dirty dishes. The only other exit from the upstairs was through a window to a vertical iron ladder fastened on the side of the building. Thank goodness there was never a fire as it would have been disastrous!

This is a photograph of the 'Hall' circa 1910. It was the meeting place for the local members of the Ancient Order of United Workmen (AOUW) and the Charter Oak Lodge before it was given to the Plainville Church to use for social events. There are apartments in the building today.

Thousands of meals were served in that old building between the early 30s and the 1960s, when the church built a new replacement fellowship hall. Ralph Bratt, an old friend, shared with me a story of how the famous Plainville Church turkey dinners originated. He stated, "In the 1930s, your dad, who grew turkeys during a time when people seldom ate turkey because of both cost and availability, was on a committee to raise money for the church." Ralph continued, "Your dad said boys, let's make some real money for the church. We'll put on a turkey dinner and charge 50 cents a person." The turkey dinner was very successful and the church has held a turkey dinner every election day with people coming from near and far. It is an event that still continues, but not for 50 cents!

Eventually ingenuity overcame the need to carry pots of gravy and platters of turkey up the stairs past diners going up and down the stairs. The installation of a dumbwaiter in the kitchen saved many steps and much of the danger created by dinner workers going up and down the stairs with food and dishes. A hole was cut in an upstairs corner of the floor, a couple of pulleys installed with a large rope connecting them to a boxlike container and by pulling hand over hand on the rope, food was moved upstairs and dirty dishes moved downstairs. Feeding a couple of hundred hungry people gave the dumbwaiter operator plenty of arm exercise!

Turkey dinners were only one of many uses for the old 'Hall'. Church functions, ice cream socials, band concerts, pit beef (beef cooked underground on hardwood coals) dinners and auctions were some of the other uses. In retrospect, the band concerts and ice cream socials were the forerunners of the drive-ins that appeared in the 1950s. They both had casual settings, satisfied an urge to eat economically away from home and provided the opportunity for interaction with neighbors and friends.

The church women prepared custard, to be churned into ice cream, for the band concerts and ice cream socials. A number of the men, women and children gathered at the church barn to freeze the custard. Salt and ice were purchased and used to encompass the cans of churning custard as the men turned the handles. As the freezer turned harder my dad would tell me to stand on top of the freezer to provide more weight and keep it steady. The best part came when we kids got the opportunity to lick the paddles after the ice cream had been frozen. That evening, when the band played, crowds came and the ice cream and other goodies were sold, was probably as enjoyable for me as going to Disney World was for my grandchildren. I often had the enjoyable task of going from car to car selling fresh popcorn for five cents a bag.

About 1950, the generosity of a community member, who had his own ice cream business, brought a night that many people in the community and myself will always remember. This gentleman offered to freeze some of the custard to make it easier for the church members and they graciously accepted his offer. Everyone who ate the ice cream that he had frozen, spent the night in their bathroom, changing from one end to the other on its previously white receptacle. I never heard how families of three or four, with only one bathroom made out! Fortunately all survived this memorable occasion.

My dad enjoyed fun and was creative in helping the church raise money. One year he went to the woods and cut a small ironwood tree, which a friend with a wood lathe turned it into facsimiles of milk bottles. People enjoyed paying a dime for the opportunity to throw three baseballs at the milk bottles and, if lucky, won a candy bar. Another time he had some willow rings made, about five inches in diameter, and people paid to throw the rings over the heads of ducks that were swimming in a tank of water. If a ring ended up around the duck's neck, they won the duck, but seldom was anyone successful. The ducks were excellent at ducking!

The old 'Hall' still rests in the same location but has been turned into three or four small apartments. If only it could talk! Think of the stories it could tell, brief snapshots of the lives of thousands of people that entered its doors for a multitude of purposes, over more than a century.

The General Store

Situated on one corner of the four-corners in Plainville, the general store was a destination for all residents living within a couple of miles. Although only about the size of a large home, it offered area residents almost everything to meet their normal needs. There was the usual line of boxed and canned foods, a butcher shop, hardware, clothing, fuel for automobile and kerosene stove, the post office and penny candy. There was always a large tree of bananas hanging near a front window and nearby cases filled with bulk cookies and crackers.

The store had originally been a hotel, which was built around 1900 after a previous hotel on the site had been destroyed by fire. Improved roads combined with the automobile removed further need for the hotel. Earl and Mary Woodruff, who had been operating a general store on South St., purchased and remodeled the hotel into a general store, which provided a better location on the four-corners.

The general store was the meeting place for everyone in the community. Mail was picked up daily, children stopped on their way to and from school, and older or unemployed men sat on a bench or the steps outside the store, passing time and exchanging stories, time which today is often spent in front of the television set. There were three or four old chairs near the back of the store to accommodate the story tellers during inclement weather.

Earl and Mary and their son Charles lived over the store. Earl and Mary were the entire staff for the store with Mary doing most of the clerking and Earl cutting the sides of beef into roasts, grinding the hamburg, stocking shelves and pumping gas. Earl was an avid hunter and took about a week each fall to hunt. When successful, his bounty

The Hotel Plainville circa 1910. It was purchased and remodeled by Earl and Mary Woodruff around 1920 and became the Plainville General Store. It was used as a store until 1991 and now serves as a private residence.

was mounted in the rear of the store. As a young boy I was awed when looking at deer heads, a moose head and especially the black bear that he returned with one year.

Each time I entered the store I looked longingly at the penny candy but seldom was allowed to have any, which made the candy even more enticing. I remember Charles reaching into one of the bulk containers to help himself to fig newtons or some other goodie and making me wish that my parents owned the store. Occasionally my mother gave me three cents, before I left for school, to buy a banana to enjoy after I had eaten my sandwiches for lunch. Some words were difficult for me to pronounce and when I told Mr. Woodruff I wanted to buy a baranna he didn't understand me so I had to point to the tree of bananas. He laughed at me and from that point on he and some of the other jokers that hung around the store gave me a new name, 'Baranna'.

A photograph of the Plainville General Store circa 1935. Notice the bench and the chairs on the porch, the sign Plainville Post Office, the kerosene pump and the Quaker State Motor Oil sign. This building was constructed as a hotel and converted to a store around 1920.

Although we butchered a cow on the farm each year, my mother occasionally purchased ground beef to serve at dinner. Mr. Woodruff walked into the cooler, rolled out a quarter of beef on the overhead rail, cut off the required amount of beef and ran it through his meat grinder. One time he demonstrated to me his enjoyment for raw beef by eating some freshly ground hamburg, something I never tried. I remember well, my mother forming the ground beef into thick patties, putting them into her cast iron frying pan that sat on the hot wood-fired kitchen stove, and turning out the best hamburg I have ever eaten.

Since the general store was the daily community meeting place, news and gossip traveled rapidly. If someone in the community was sick or a death occurred, Mary willingly accepted contributions from neighbors and friends to help the person in need.

West of the store was a small building that served as an ice cream stand during the summer months. It served hot dogs, hamburgers, milk shakes and sundaes along with five and ten cent ice cream cones. It was my favorite spot in the community, probably because we enjoyed it so seldom. One year, I remember my dad giving me 50 cents to buy my lunch on my birthday. Lucy Hawker worked in the stand and I can still remember the juicy hamburger and the delicious chocolate milk shake she served me for lunch on that special day. Few people had a freezer in their home and seldom had ice cream, making the stand a special spot.

There was about an acre of good fertile land behind the store where the Woodruff's grew vegetables to sell in the store during the summer and fall. Eggs, strawberries, raspberries and cherries were obtained from people who had extra to sell or trade and then sold in the store. There wasn't a shorter trip from farm to market other than from a homeowner's garden to the kitchen stove, a marked contrast to the thousands of miles that fruits and vegetables travel today!

Eventually, as the automobile came into greater use, many of the Plainville area customers bought the bulk of their needs from the bigger stores that were beginning to appear in the larger villages, buying only fill-in items at the general store. Earl and Mary reached retirement age and sold the store to a new owner. The general store lost many of its customers, the post office moved to a new location and the general store gradually lost its prominence in the community. In 1991, the general store closed and now serves only as a residence for its owner. Although the general store has gone, it is not totally forgotten. Earl and Mary Woodruff and their general store still bring warm memories to those of us who walked through its doors many years ago.

Plainville School

An overturned kerosene light in the house next to the school brought a happy day for the children attending the Plainville school as it disappeared in flames. Their joy was short lived as school continued in a local lodge while a new two-room school was built, and ready for the students in 1921. Construction costs and bonding to pay for the school were different at that time. A prosperous local farmer bought the eight $1,000 bonds, that paid for the entire cost of the school. Funds to pay for the bonds were raised by taxes on the local district with one bond retired each year over an eight year period.

The first school, a log building also used as a church was constructed in 1819. In 1841 a frame school replaced the log cabin and in 1874 a three room 10 grade brick school was constructed. This building was used until it was destroyed in the previously mentioned fire of 1920.

Thanks to the earlier fire my school days began when the school was only 15 years old. Each teacher had four grades of approximately five children. As the teacher called a grade for their lessons in the front of the room, those of us remaining had the opportunity to have an early start to learn the lessons of a future grade or to review the lessons we had in the past. Usually the teachers lived in the community and knew both the children and their parents. Most of the parents told their children that if they were punished by their teacher their punishment at home would be even more severe. The students believed the teacher had a rubber hose to apply when behavior was bad but I never saw it used. It probably was only a rumor but served as a strong deterrent.

The school had a belfry containing a large cast iron bell. A heavy rope attached to the bell hung down over the stairway into the school. The children were all tempted to give a good pull on the rope as they walked by but that only happened at the end of the school day if one of the teachers wasn't watching. The teacher used the bell to call us to class mornings, noon and after recess.

That school bell became close to me again in about 1988 when the Plainville Fire Department gave me the bell for use at the Plainville Turkey Farm Visitor Center. I mounted it next to the visitor center, attached a rope to the bell and gave thousands of schoolchildren visiting the farm, the opportunity to ring and hear the clanging of the old school bell. I rang the bell 100 times when the year 2000 arrived. In 2010, I gave the bell back to the Fire Department, hoping they might install it at the firehouse, since I no longer had a worthy use for it.

The Plainville School circa 1900. It housed grades 1 to 10. It was constructed in 1874 and burned in 1920. The Plainville Fire Department is located on the site at this time. Courtesy of Marilyn Hollenbeck

A circa 1907 photo of the students attending the Plainville School, which housed grades 1-10. A few familiar names starting on the left in the back row are Ralph Huntington, Ruth Ward - teacher, Emmet Clark - Principal, Blanch Calkins, Edna Hotaling, Annie Smith - teacher, Ruby Fowler, Clara Scott, Maude Bitz, Vida Pickard, Rufus Gates, Robert Burghduff, Frank Carncross, John Chase, Lewis Davis. Some of the other student's last names in the photo are Duger, Tillotson, Upson, Dunham, Johnson, Knowlton, Reed, Voorhees, Gates, Wilson, Cox, Tabor, and Pelton. Perhaps you can pick out a grandparent or family relative of yours.

The school was on three levels; the entrance was at ground level, the classrooms were about eight steps higher and the rest rooms eight steps down. Extending beyond the rest rooms was the furnace, fed by a coal stoker. The rest of the basement provided a stormy day, inside play area for the release of the children's pent-up energy that gradually developed while they sat at their desks. The play area was Spartan, with only a seven foot ceiling, concrete floor and concrete walls but the imagination and ingenuity of the children created a variety of active games.

Most of the time, snow sleet or rain didn't deter the more active children from using their energy in outdoor activities on the large playground. Football, and baseball with a rubber ball, arrived during the appropriate seasons, with snowball fights in the winter, marbles in the

The two room school in Plainville was constructed in 1921 at a total cost of a little less than $8,000. It was closed as a school around 1958 and sold to the Plainville Fire Department for a dollar. It was used as a children's community center for a few years and then for fire department meetings until it succumbed to the wrecking ball in 2010.

spring and a variety of active games interspersed throughout the school year.

Every child walked to school. They came from all four directions, in ones, twos or in groups, from a few hundred feet to two or three miles. They came from both farms and rural homes. Bad weather wasn't a consideration, although a few times, when it was especially snowy, my dad invited the children living on our road to jump on the bobs, pulled by a team of horses, for a ride to school. The fact that he had previously taken our farm's daily livestock organic fertilizer production to the field on the bobs, bothered none of us.

The County Health Nurse stopped by a couple of times a year to check for head lice while keeping an eye open for potential contagious illnesses. The County Superintendent of Schools stopped twice a year to observe the teachers, especially if a teacher was new. When the Superintendent was present, the children were on especially good behavior. A music teacher stopped for an hour every month with the intent of teaching the students some of the finer aspects of music, but with feeble success.

Country folk, during the 1930s, ignored the separation of church and state. Every two weeks the school welcomed the pastor of the local church for a prayer, hymn sing and a short message. The children presented a Christmas pageant in the church each year since it was the only facility in the area large enough to accommodate proud parents, brothers and sisters, grandparents and cousins. Regardless of their faith or lack of faith, all were welcome.

Plainville School District was one of more than a dozen rural districts that sent their children to Baldwinsville Academy for a high school education at the end of the 8th grade. All 8th graders had to pass several New York State Regent examinations before going to Baldwinsville. This was an additional incentive for the teachers to have the children well prepared. To the surprise of many people, the children from the rural schools tended to outperform the children who had eight grades and kindergarten at the Baldwinsville Academy. Apparently the old-fashioned country schools didn't do a bad job teaching their students!

The last day of the school year was celebrated with a school picnic at an amusement park on Owasco Lake, about 25 miles from the school. There were a variety of fun rides including the traditional merry-go-round, roller coaster and even a fun house. This was the favorite day of the school year for the youngsters.

The two-room country school in Plainville became a part of the past in about 1958 when it was closed. Ten years earlier it had become a part of the Baldwinsville Central School. The school board decided that the children could obtain a better education in the much larger school in Baldwinsville. Instead of walking to school each day, the children boarded a bus and rode seven miles to school. The cohesiveness of the community created by the country school was gradually lost, and it now became a community of strangers living in the same locality but unknown to each other.

The old school property was sold to the local fire department for one dollar, and was used by the fire department for meetings and small social functions. Laws were passed requiring public buildings to have handicap accessible facilities and the building no longer could be used without excessive remodeling expenditures. In 2010, the school succumbed to the wrecking ball and all that remains are the memories of the students who received a good start in life, thanks to the little two-room school.

A 1932 picture of grades 1-4 in the Plainville School. No names are listed but the teacher was Ada Vreeland and the author recognizes Arthur Gates and Ruth Charlotte Bitz. Courtesy of Marilyn Hollenbeck

A Little Plainville School History

The official minute book of Plainville School meetings provides a glimpse of the past that would otherwise be forgotten. Its records extend from 1881to 1945. The records are minimal but provide a view of the gradual changes taking place in rural education.

In 1883, the two teachers in the Plainville School were paid an average of $7.50 a week for the 18 week winter term and an average of $5.75 a week for the 18 week summer term. In 1905, the teachers were still earning about $230 a year but by 1932 it had increased to about $1,100 a year and in 1945 had reached $1,300.

 No dates are given for the beginning and end of each term but the school year ended on September 30 in 1883, which indicates the actual time of the terms may have been winter and summer. The school terms probably changed in 1884 as the annual meeting was held on August 26. In 1889, the school year ended on July 25 and in 1910 the school year ended August 1. Beginning in 1911, the annual school meetings were held in early May so it is likely that the school year was ending in June at that time.

In 1883, the district received $224.19 in state aid and raised $352.70 in taxes. The assessed valuation of the district was $229,215 making the tax rate about $1.57 per thousand assessment. There were 108 children in the district eligible for school but only 58 attended at any time during the year. Of those attending the average attendance was less than 50%. Apparently school attendance was taken more seriously by 1906, as an attendance officer was appointed and reimbursed $6 a year. A few of the expenses during 1883 were 60 cents for two brooms, two dippers five cents each, six erasers for a total of 90 cents and a box of chalk for 20 cents. The following year 16 books, at a total cost of $7, were purchased for the school's library.

In 1901, it was voted that Plainville become a regents school and that $180 be raised for that purpose. (The author is suspicious that this was the time when grades nine and ten became part of the school's offerings.) It also voted to become a Union Free School. At the same meeting it was voted that students from outside the district be charged $4 for tuition in the lower room and $6 in the upper room. They also resolved that the school grounds should be mowed at least twice a year and that the trustees should construct a drilled well on the school grounds. The search for water could not have been successful because in 1916, a resolution was passed for the trustees to make arrangements to obtain water for the school. (The author remembers carrying pails of water for drinking from the house across the road in 1940, because the school water wasn't good.) Water must have been located because in 1919 there was an expenditure of $170 for two toilets that probably brought about the end of the outhouses.

Calamity hit in 1920 when a fire from the house to the east spread to the school, which was destroyed. The insurance paid $1,500 for the building and $500 for its fixtures. At a special meeting it was resolved to rent the AOUW building for the 1920-21 school year for $150.

On April 29,1921 at a special meeting, the district, by a vote of 28 to 1, authorized the sale of eight $1,000 bonds, one to be paid each year for eight years from money to be raised by taxes. A month later the bid of the only bidder, Edmund Turner was accepted at 6% interest. Interestingly, in 1882 Edmund Turner had been one of the students in the school, which was destroyed 38 years later. The total cost of building the new school was$7,801.50. A number of the men living in the local community were employed in constructing the school.

On May 2,1933 the school district voted to provide transportation for academic students to the Baldwinsville High School. It also voted not to provide transportation for any elementary students. Two years later the district voted to have the trustees build a fence along the main highway next to the school. In 1938, it was voted to increase the school janitor's salary from $125 a year to $200 and the following year it was voted that the school day was to begin at 9:00 a.m.

The author remembers considerable discussion in the early 1940s whether to send the district's children to Cato or Baldwinsville. Cato had recently constructed a magnificent new school and had extra room. In 1944, the Plainville district voted to provide transportation for high school students to both Baldwinsville and Cato but the following year only authorized transportation to Baldwinsville.

The teachers are only occasionally named in the school's minutes. Some that are mentioned were Ada Vreeland who taught grades one to four from 1929 to 1939 and Charlotte Bitz who taught grades five through eight from 1929 to 1940. Gladys Carrington taught grades one through four from 1940 though 1945. During the author's fifth through eighth grades he had Helen Mount one year followed by Norma Wallbridge two years and Clare Green the last year.

The Blacksmith Shop

For well over 100 years, ever since it was first settled, residents of the hamlet of Plainville could hear the sound of the blacksmith's hammer clanging, as it shaped red hot iron on his anvil. His powerful arm moved up and down fashioning or repairing objects of iron needed by some member of the community. Almost everyone in a rural community, from the time it was first settled until into the 1900s, relied upon the blacksmith. The blacksmith was needed to repair anything made of iron and, depending upon his skill, make almost any iron object needed.

In the early 1800s, the blacksmith made a great variety of necessities including nails, bolts, horseshoes and sometimes even wagons and carriages. By the 1930s, when I first was in the blacksmith shop, fewer members of the community needed his services, which had dwindled to primarily shoeing horses. Fred Pickard was Plainville's last blacksmith and operated his shop from about the 1910s to the 1950s.

Mr. Pickard's blacksmith shop was in the walkout basement of his home on one of the corners of the Plainville four-corners kitty-corner from the general store. There were two garage size doors leading into it, one from the North and one from the East. These doors provided the shop with good natural lighting and natural ventilation. The shop was an area of 20 by 30 feet, providing room for his forge, anvil, tools and sufficient room to shoe a team of horses or build a wagon.

The focal points of any blacksmith shop are the forge, in one corner of the shop, with the anvil a few feet away. Red hot iron from the forge, held by tongs in one hand, was pounded into the desired shape with the hammer in his other hand. Sparks flew across the shop floor as the

Fred Pickard standing in the door of his blacksmith shop facing Route 370 in Plainville circa 1920. Courtesy of Kaye Forsythe

hammer struck the iron. Coal was burned in the forge to heat the iron, and a bellows, mounted nearby on the ceiling, was used to blow air on the fire, increasing the fire's temperature and heating the iron to the desired color. Tongs were used to position the iron in the appropriate spot in the fire. Occasionally Mr. Pickard removed the iron from the fire, examining its color, to determine if the appropriate temperature had been reached.

The greater part of Mr. Pickard's work was shoeing horses for the neighboring farmers. In earlier days of blacksmithing, horseshoes were shaped from a flat bar of iron but by the middle of the 1800s partially shaped horseshoes were purchased by the blacksmith with the curve of the horse's foot and nail holes already in place. There were several different sizes of shoes so the blacksmith could choose the one closest to the size of the horse's foot.

My dad used to make an appointment to have horses shod and, since we only lived a half-mile away, I often led the horses to the blacksmith shop. It was an awesome experience for a young boy to watch the iron heated, the sparks fly as the shoe was pounded on the anvil, smell the searing hoof as the shoe was placed against it to determine if it had reached the necessary shape. I marveled as the blacksmith picked up the horse's foot, held the horse's hoof between his legs and drove nails with a hammer through the shoe, into the hoof and then clinch the ends of the nails extending through the hoof. It amazed me that it never hurt the horse. I also enjoyed hearing the hissing of the water and watching the steam rise up as he cooled the shoe in a tub of water before nailing it to the horse's foot. I still wonder how many of the odors, from the searing horses hooves and the manure that inevitably came from the horses, floated through the ceiling into the upstairs rooms in the house. Probably the Pickards, like myself working with turkeys, accepted the odor as one of the necessities of the business.

As the need for blacksmith services decreased in the 1920s, Mr. Pickard began selling farm machinery to help maintain his business. He did this for a number of years but eventually larger dealers, that had trained mechanics and who could offer a broader range of machinery and services, ended the days of the small dealer. Mr. Pickard continued shoeing horses occasionally until the 1950s retiring after a lifetime of service to the community.

The blacksmith shop was of an era when an item was made, one at a time, by an individual whom you knew. The item was seldom thrown away but was repaired for unending use. It was an era of the proud craftsman who could take a lump of iron and turn it into a special object that served the specific needs of each person. That era has given way to mass production, limited pride in workmanship and a throw-it-away society. It was an era that will never come back but one that gives me fond memories.

The Plainville Fire Department

U ndoubtedly the beginnings of a fire department occurred when the second family settled in the Plainville area. There was an innate code, in all early settlements, of helping your neighbor in time of need. Every member of the community was an unofficial member of a non-existing fire department and when an emergency arose immediately went to the aid of his neighbor. If the emergency was a fire, he grabbed a couple of buckets and raced to help put the fire out. As neighbors came running with buckets, a bucket brigade was formed, with each person passing a pail of water to the next to fight the rampaging fire.

In the Plainville area, even though buildings were not built close to each other the danger of the fire spreading to nearby buildings was real and much of the effort during a fire was to wet the roofs of adjacent buildings to prevent the blaze from spreading. Once a fire had much of a start it was difficult to extinguish by just throwing pails of water on it.

The Plainville Fire Department was officially formed in 1922. A $1,000 bond was floated and the money was used to purchase a Ford Model T truck, a gasoline powered pump and some hose. A few 10 gallon milk cans filled with water were kept on the back of the truck. The equipment was stored in Fred Pickard's blacksmith shop until the next year when a small concrete block garage was constructed next to the blacksmith shop. Since Mr. Pickard, the local blacksmith, was usually working next door, he was the unofficial fire chief. If someone had a fire they called the Pickard residence, Mrs. Pickard yelled downstairs to her husband and he set off the fire siren. Men in the village came running, jumped into the pickup truck and headed to the fire. Hopefully, on arrival at the fire, there would be water near the site and the pump would start. I remember going to a fire once and watching the men take the pump to the nearby Seneca River but, sadly, the pump wouldn't start.

Early one evening, in about 1936, the cow barn on my dad's farm, filled with hay, was struck by lightning. My dad ran to the barn with a pail of water while my mother called the Pickards to sound the fire alarm. Dad climbed into the hay mow and was able to contain the fire until the fire truck and neighbors arrived. The fire was extinguished with minimal damage to the barn. For many years the scorched boards on the side of the barn were a reminder how near our barn had come to being nothing but a pile of ashes.

After World War II an active volunteer fire department was formed in Plainville and in 1950, a used military surplus fire truck from the Mattydale Airbase was purchased. About the same time, the Plainville

A 2012 photograph of the first Plainville Fire House built in 1922. The building directly behind the firehouse was Fred Pickard's blacksmith shop.

Fire Department bought additional property next to the old firehouse, built a new firehouse and purchased additional modern equipment. With a relatively modern piece of equipment, it was necessary for the fire department members to have training in order to operate the equipment effectively and care for it properly.

Membership in the Plainville Fire Department increased, and organized social activities began to be connected with the department. The department participated in parades, had field days and formed a ladies' auxiliary. Two satellite fire houses were constructed to minimize the time required to reach a fire.

 As an outgrowth of these activities, in 1960, a hearse was donated, overhauled and put into use to provide emergency medical service in the community. It was a continuation of the policy of neighbor helping neighbor. Later, technicians were trained, and a modern ambulance and rescue unit were purchased.

When the Plainville School closed in the 1960s, it was sold to the Plainville Fire Department for one dollar and used for a few years as a recreation center for area children. Later the old schoolhouse was used for fire department meetings and in 1996, a large modern firehouse was constructed on the old school property.

With Plainville becoming increasingly more of a bedroom community, coupled with strict government regulations, membership in the Plainville Fire Department and almost all other volunteer fire departments in the area is decreasing. There may come a time when Plainville will become part of a regional fire department with a paid staff.

Neighbors, often not knowing each other and no longer dependent upon each other during emergencies, now rely on government agencies to take care of many of their needs. This change comes at a cost not only in dollars but also in the community spirit.

Hundreds of Plainville area residents have donated thousands of hours of their time helping their neighbors during times of emergency. They answered many calls during the night, that interrupted their sleep after a busy day. They put their lives at risk helping each other. The volunteer members of the Plainville Fire Department have performed dedicated service to their community for many years and are continuing to do so in a time of increasingly challenging changes.

A Little History of Plainville's Businesses and Public Buildings

L ike all small hamlets of Upstate New York, established in the early 19th century, there were a variety of businesses in Plainville to take care of the majority of the needs of people living within two or three miles. Although there was probably a blacksmith and a general store earlier, the construction of a log schoolhouse, which occurred in 1819, was the first business or public building recorded. The log school was replaced with a frame building in 1841 and that one was replaced by a 10 grade two-story brick school in 1874.

The Plainville Post Office has a 'moving' history. Letters were left in a hollow tree south of Plainville before an actual post office came into existence in the same general area. As postmasters came and went, the post office moved to their residence or place of business. The author remembers the post office in Woodruff's store, then in the garage across the street and later in the residence of Edith Forsythe on South St. In the later part of the 1970s, the Plainville Post Office received a permanent home on the east side of Plainville Rd. at the outskirts of the village. There is more information concerning the schools, churches and various buildings in other chapters.

Lyman Norton, an eminent Plainville resident, opened a dry goods store in 1831. He served several terms as Supervisor of the Town of Lysander, was postmaster for many years and a member of the New York State Assembly. Mr. Norton's home was on the west side of South St. and is currently owned by Bruce and Sue McManus. He provided land for the Plainville Cemetery and operated it as a private cemetery until 1897 when it became the Plainville Rural Cemetery Association.

Mr. Norton, along with A.R. Jaycox, was one of the owners of the Plainville Cheese Mfg. Co., which was founded in 1872. Four years later the cheese factory was destroyed by fire. An article in the November 24,1876 Syracuse Journal indicated that arson was the probable cause.

One of Lyman Norton's sons, J.H., was also a businessman and published a small monthly newspaper called the Plainville Moniter. He also headed a company that purchased 10 acres of land known as the 'Old Wilson Place' with the intent of drilling for salt. There had been an old 'deer lick' on the property where they drilled. According to the April 1,1864 Gazette, (the author doubts that it was a newspaper April Fool joke and suspects that J.H. was the one fooled with no salt discovered) a drill house had been constructed and machinery for boring the well had been set up.

Peter Voorhees came to Plainville in 1813 and died three years later. His son, Colonel J. L. Voorhees, was a very successful businessman and became known in wide circles as the 'tall pine of Plainville'. He purchased substantial amounts of land, constructed barns on a number of sites and then sold the farms to settlers. These barns were of an unusual style with the barn floor extending beyond the basement wall about five feet on one side. There are still several continuing to be used today.

Colonel Voorhees owned a log boring company in Baldwinsville, constructed the bridge over the Seneca River at New Bridge (now called Belgium) and even had the contract to build large ocean docks in New York City. He served as an assemblyman and was a member of the Whig party. He built the large brick home on Rt. 370 east of Plainville in 1833, where he entertained a variety of distinguished visitors including Henry Clay. Unfortunately, a magnificent large Dutch barn he constructed on his farm was not maintained and collapsed in the 1960s. This was the only Dutch barn constructed west of Utica.

Other Plainville businesses were a tannery constructed in 1860 on the west side of Plainville Rd. a little north of Sprague Rd., a wagon shop built in 1833 and several shoemakers' shops that existed over the years. There was a notable article in the March 25,1864 Syracuse Journal, which stated, "Andrew H. Green a shoemaker in Plainville was found guilty of maintaining a gaming house and fined $50. He is to remain in jail until the fine is paid."

One of the larger Plainville businesses was Ebenezer Allen's carriage and wagon manufacturing business. It was located on South St. just north of the octagon house approximately where the Ancient Order of United Workman, later the home of the Charter Oak Lodge and still later the church 'Hall' was constructed. A March 19, 1879 article in the Courier tells about the fire that destroyed the carriage business and several other buildings.

"At about half-past five o'clock last Saturday afternoon, Mr. Wm. Scott and Dr. Sullivan noticed that the roof of the wood shop of Ebenezer Allen's carriage manufactory was on fire. Ladders were speedily procured and an effort made to extinguish the flames, but it became evident in the course of five minutes that the fire was beyond control, and efforts were at once made to save such property as could be moved. The schoolhouse and church bells were rung, the inhabitants of the village, old and young, male and female, all turned out to render such assistance as they could. Within an hour the extensive manufactory of Mr. Allen's was totally destroyed, wagon shop, paint and trimming shop, blacksmith shop, and barns adjacent; he succeeded in saving about fifty wagons, completed and in various stages of construction, together with a few tools, and a small amount of stock; his loss he estimates as being about $5,000; insured for $2,000. The fire extended to the blacksmith shop of Mr. John Scott, situated just north, which was totally consumed. Mr. Scott succeeded in saving his tools and most of his stock; his loss is estimated at $600; insured for $400. Mr Hugh Sample who lived in the rooms over the blacksmith shop succeeded in removing most of his household goods. The office of Dr. Schenck, now occupied by R.B. Sullivan, M.D., was several times on fire, and the clap boarding burned through in several places, but was finally saved. Dr. B.B. Schenck's fine octagon barn was consumed. Eight buildings were destroyed. The total loss is nearly $7,000 and is a severe blow to the industries of this little hamlet. Mr. Allen proposes to move his business to Baldwinsville with as little delay as possible, and has already taken measures to procure a suitable building."

There were numerous fires in Plainville over the years, which was typical of most villages throughout New York. A church, a school, a hotel, a tavern, an occasional house and several barns were destroyed by fire at various times. Buildings were heated by wood and there was no fire fighting equipment or fire department until 1922.

Some other Plainville businesses were two basket makers, a planing and molding business and a sawmill. From the 1950s to the 1990s, Stachurski Brothers operated a sawmill on Rt. 370 at the end of Tater Road. A creamery was constructed on the south side of the road and east of the four-corners in Plainville some time after the cheese factory burned. The creamery discontinued operations with the advent of motor trucks and improved roads.

The big Plainville industry from about 1860 to the early 1900s was tobacco. There were three tobacco warehouses in Plainville and three cigar manufacturers. One warehouse was west of Plainville, approximately across from the church. The building served as a service station in the 1940s and was later destroyed. Another tobacco warehouse was south of Plainville on the William Wilson farm. This was converted into a feed storage building by Plainville Turkey Farm in 1953 and demolished in the 1980s.

The first commercial building the author remembers constructed in Plainville was a garage and gas station across from the store and slightly west of the four-corners, by Smith Cooper in about 1938. The building was used as a service station until the late 1900s. A gas station was built east of the four-corners on the south side of Rt. 370 in the 1950s. It later was used as a dealership for the French made Citroen automobile and currently is an auto repair shop.

Undoubtedly, with more research, additional businesses and public buildings could be located. We do know that the Plainville area community was largely self-sufficient for more than a century as residents who saw a need stepped forward to provide the desired services.

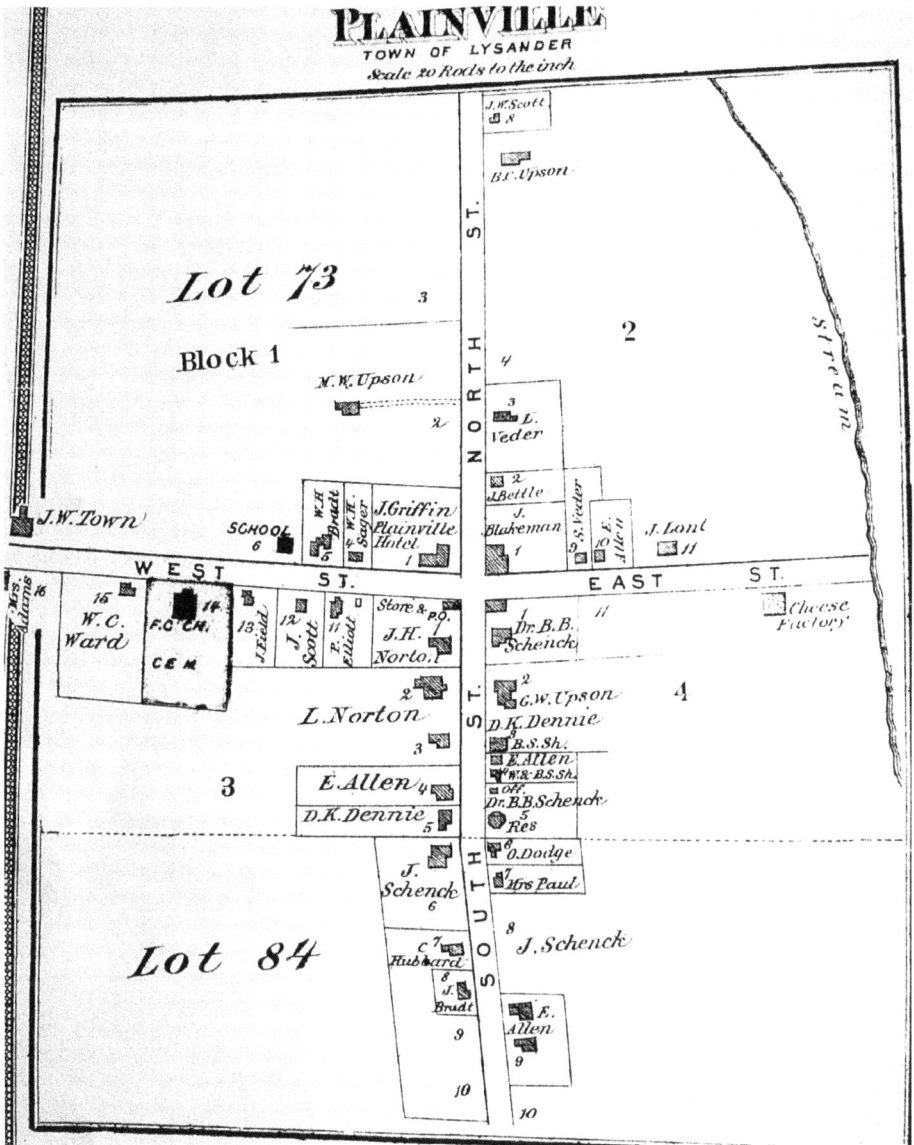

An 1874 map of Plainville by Homer D.L. Sweet shows the residences and public buildings in existence at that time.

A circa 1918 photo of Hattie Bitz, Maude Bitz and Irving Bitz in front of their home on West St. between the general store and the school. Notice the bicycle on the porch. Bicycles were a common means of transportation at this time.

Plainville residence of Dr. B.B. Schenck. It comes from a lithograph in W.W. Clayton's 1878 History of Onondaga County. The octagon house remains but the octagon carriage house burned in a fire in 1879 and Dr. Schenck's office is gone.

This circa 1959 photo is of children enjoying a ride on a set of bobs behind Harry Bitz's team of horses. Some of the children are Frances Green, Albert and Robert Dettbarn, Janice Bartoszewski, Lois, Louise and Jean Gates.

The Plainville home of Lyman Norton is on the left and the home of his son J.H. Norton is the middle building. The building on the right had been Lyman Norton's store but when this lithograph was done in 1878 the store belonged to J.H. Norton. All three buildings are easily identified today. From W.W. Clayton's History of Onondaga County.

A photo of the Plainville House circa 1880. This hotel burned in 1898 and was replaced by a smaller hotel that was later remodeled into a general store. Notice the open doors on the far end of the hotel for the storage of carriages and sleighs of the guests. There was a separate hitching barn just beyond the end of the building. Notice the pump in the lower right and the water tub where people could water their horses. The photo shows what looks like steam, smoke or dust coming from two of the upper windows.

20th Anniversary of the Charter Oak Lodge

PROGRAM
1927

Toastmistress—MISS MAUDE BITZ

Gleanings from the Baldwinsville Gazette of
Twenty Years Ago.

MR. HARLAN GATES

Horse Power Today and Twenty Years Ago.

MRS. HAROLD MEAKER

Amusements and Customs—Today and
Twenty Years Ago.

MRS. GROVE SMITH

Developments of Science in the Past Twenty
Years.

MR. HARRY BITZ

What Science May Accomplish in the Next
Twenty Years.

MISS MABEL BRATT

*One page of the program for the 20th Anniversary celebration, in
1927, of the Charter Oak Lodge.*

*(right) This circa 1910 picture of the
Loomis & DeLyne general store was
located on Plainville's four-corners
directly across from the Plainville Hotel.
This building had been a store operated
by the Norton family during most of
the 1800s. It has served as a private
residence for the last 75 years.*

This is a 2008 photo of the house built by Colonel James L. Voorhees in 1833. It is located on Route 370 a half mile east of Plainville. It was originally called 'Whig Hill' because of the political affiliation of Colonel Voorhees and the members of the Whig party who used to meet there.

Loomis & DeLyne's Store, Plainville, N. Y.

The tobacco warehouse, sorting room and cigar manufacturing building, circa 1920, on West St., across from the church. Courtesy of Virginia Billings

Honor Roll

ROBERT E POTTER	EARL M TIMMERMAN	RUTH A CONNERS
ROBERT L PICKARD	ADRAIN BROEKHUIZEN	LISLE BRATT
ALLEN N TIMMERMAN	RAYMOND DAVENPORT	ROBERT FORDERKONS
LLOYD THOMAS	ELMER DAVENPORT	CURTIS H ROOT
HAROLD REAUME	DONALD B COOLIDGE	CHARLES R VICTORY
JOSEPH R PATCHETT	MAURICE D BRATT	BERNARD E BOND
CARLTON F PICKARD	JOHN ISHAM	KENNETH L WOODRUFF
LLEWELLYN T PICKARD	D SHERLEY MATTESON	ROBERT E TREXLER
ROBERT ADSIT	G GRENVILLE FLATT	VERNARD MANN
LISLE M PICKARD	WILLIAM A TREXLER	DOUGLAS H REID
DONALD N PICKARD	GEORGE CONIBER	MERLE MILLIMAN
PAUL N BLAIR	CHARLES R WOODRUFF	MILTON ADSIT
CHARLES M THOMAS	CLIFFORD TIMMERSON JR	WILLIAM L RICHARDSON
JACK RAY	FLOYD B REISTROM	CLIFFORD H SCHAEFER
CARL O REISTROM	ELMER E SCHAEFER	

Llewellyn Pickard standing by the list of World War II soldiers from the Plainville area. More names may have been added later in the war and stars were later added for at least two of the men who were killed in the war. The Honor Roll was located just east of the general store next to Plainville Road.

Thinking Back on a Few Memorable Community Members

Every community has what are commonly referred to as characters. This, however, is about people with whom I had positive interactions as a young man.

Reverend D. Cecil Flatt came with his wife and their youngest four children to Plainville in about 1939. He served the Plainville Christian Church as Pastor for about a decade. He was the type of person that everyone loved and was a tireless worker helping the people in the community. Because the church was poor, his pay was meager, but he always had a positive attitude. After he retired, he became Pastor Emeritus and lived in the community until his death. At Thanksgiving and Christmas he helped my dad prepare turkeys for sale and while working joked and had an enjoyable time with the other workers.

Glenn Bratt was a farmer who lived nearby and had three fine sons. As the sons became old enough to do the morning livestock chores, Glenn volunteered to take dressed turkeys to the Syracuse Regional Market at Thanksgiving and Christmas. Another farm neighbor, Harold Meaker, also volunteered to help. My dad assigned me to go to market and help them. The three of us went to market together for several years, from the time I was 11 and until I went to college. Although I was just a young boy they treated me with respect and I had the opportunity to learn a great deal about working with people through these experiences. They were both very fine men and I am thankful for their friendship. Amazingly, some years later my oldest son Mark was also able to take turkeys to the market with Mr. Bratt. Glenn was President of the Plainville Rural Cemetery Association at a time when the Association had little money. He voluntarily walked behind a power mower, mowing the cemetery for several years with no renumeration. The cemetery covered two acres and about as soon as it was mowed it was time to start up again. Glenn Bratt was an example of dedication and selflessness working at an age when few people half of his age would have been willing to accomplish what he did.

Herbert Voorhees (Pat) was another neighbor. As a young man Pat lost one hand in an accident but continued working on his farm, more capably than many men with both hands. What he was able to accomplish with one hand was a great inspiration. Our farm used a great deal of water for growing and processing turkeys but never could find a good source of good water. Pat let me drill for water on his farm and told me he would sell me the land if I secured the necessary water. True to his word, we found a good supply of water and he sold me the land at a fair price. I will always be thankful for the fine examples he set.

Fred Potter (Paddy) lived on one of the corners of the four-corners of Plainville. As a younger man he had worked as a hired man for my grandfather and lived in the house, that I later lived in, with his family. When I knew him he worked for farmers by the day or week and helped my dad with the turkeys at Thanksgiving and Christmas. Paddy was a hardworking man who chewed tobacco and loved to tell stories. He once told me, "Every night before I go to bed I put a chew of tobacco in my mouth and keep it there all night without ever getting anything on the pillow!" Another time when I was only about seven and from a family that would never go near a drop of alcohol, he said to me, "I like beer like a cat likes milk!" Naturally I was shocked. Later on, for an entire year, Paddy helped a local carpenter, Roy Woodruff, repairing several barns and a house on a run-down farm my dad had purchased. They had dinner with our family that year and I gained increased respect for Fred.

I am thankful for the opportunity to have known dozens of other fine people in the Plainville community. A community becomes what it is because of its residents and Plainville had many good people. None were what could be considered wealthy but most were hardworking, honest and always willing to help someone in need.

Farm

Our Farm

Originally, when great-great grandfather bought our farm in 1835 it contained 72 acres,. In the 1890s, grandfather added another 24 acres making it slightly larger than the average New York State farm. About 60 acres were tillable with the remaining land woodlot, permanent pasture, orchard and farm buildings. With both livestock and crops it was large enough to provide a reasonable living for two families.

Initially the main cash crop was wheat with tobacco added in the 1850s and potatoes around 1900. These crops provided the necessary money to pay the taxes and to purchase farm and home needs. Farms in the 1800s were largely self-sufficient with relatively little money changing hands.

The 1865 New York State Census provides an accurate account of the farm's livestock and crop production during the previous year, which was similar to the hundreds of other similar farms in the area. There were eight acres of wheat that yielded 250 bushels, eight acres of barley producing 105 bushels, six acres of Indian corn yielding 75 bushels, four acres of oats yielding 116 bushels, one-half acre of buckwheat producing eight bushels, a half acre of potatoes furnishing 70 bushels and an acre of tobacco yielding 500 pounds. There were 52 apple trees producing 150 bushels and four barrels of cider. Four cows produced 300 pounds of butter and 100 pounds of cheese. Three pigs furnished 800 pounds of pork, 19 sheep provided 70 pounds of wool and $6 was received from chicken eggs that were sold.

There were three horses and the value of farm tools and equipment was $75. One sheep was killed by dogs and $3 of fertilizer was purchased. The total value of the livestock was $300 and the 72 acre farm with buildings was valued at $4,000.

Aerial view of Plainville Turkey Farm (Bitz farm) Circa 1951. Large barn in back next to silo held horses, cows, potato cellar, granary, hay mow, and wheat mow. Smaller barn by road held cows and was the one struck by lightning in 1936. Long dark barn was the tobacco shed with stripping room where turkeys were dressed for market for over 25 years. The upper building with the metal roof was built in 1950 to dress turkeys. Harry and Metta Bitz lived in the near house and a hired man lived in the other house. Notice the woodpiles of wood drying, in the center, to be used for heating the houses the next year. There are two turkey brooder houses with turkeys on their sun porches in the foreground.

Not mentioned in the census were the acres of hay and pasture that furnished the feed for the farm livestock or a large garden and additional fruit trees that furnished much of the food for the two families on the farm.

Milk was sold to the creamery, when it came to Plainville in the early 1900s, and the dairy herd increased to eight or nine cows. Starting in 1923, the farm began raising some turkeys and about the same time discontinued chickens. Tobacco production was discontinued in the early 30s because of extremely low prices but returned to the farm for a few years in 1940 when the price of tobacco had substantially increased. When a pea vinery was constructed, a mile north of Plainville, a few acres of peas were grown.

With the arrival of a tractor in 1939, the farm slowly expanded. Land was rented from other farmers to gradually increase the acres of crops grown. In 1943, Dad bought an adjacent 90 acre farm. A few more cows were added but the dairy herd never reached more than 20 milkers. A year later he bought another nearby 40 acre farm and by 1944 was farming 300 acres, half of it tillable. Dad was now growing cabbage and red kidney beans as well as increased acres of corn, oats and wheat.

World War II brought a strong demand for farm products and with it, higher prices. All farmers, including my dad, attempted to increase production. Farm machinery was becoming larger but was difficult to obtain because farm machinery manufacturers had re-tooled for the war effort. Agriculture was beginning major long term changes. Few people were able to foresee the extent of the change, and farmers who didn't move forward with changes soon found another occupation.

Turkeys on our farm are part of another story but became a greater part of our farm business as years passed. The cash crops were gradually discontinued and the cows were sold in the 1960s. Now the farm relied

House constructed in 1882 where Bob Bitz grew up.

only on the sale of turkeys for its income. Corn acreage increased and soybeans were introduced to the farm, both used as feed for the turkeys. Because of the cost of modern machinery, specialization in agriculture became necessary to compete effectively and return a profit. On our farm it became evident by the late 1940s that turkeys would be the best choice. I enjoyed the turkey business and felt that growing and marketing turkeys would bring the greatest success.

Family Life

We were a multi generational family composed of my maternal grandparents, parents, older sister and epileptic aunt. In addition, family relatives or friends often visited for a few days or weeks, making an interesting and active family life.

We lived in the house my grandparents had built when they were married, about 50 years earlier. Less than 100 feet away, across our driveway was the house where grandfather had been born, built by his grandfather in 1835. It was a family farm and our roots grew deep.

Most of what we ate was grown on the farm. There was a huge garden with a great variety of vegetables. In addition, we had apples, cherries, pears, strawberries, raspberries, currents and rhubarb. Mother and Grandmother canned hundreds of quarts of fruit, vegetables and even canned pork and beef at slaughter time. My aunt cracked hickory and butternuts by the hour, embellishing the cakes and cookies we enjoyed on a daily basis. Bread was baked twice weekly. How was I to know that I was born and growing up during the 'Great Depression'!

The woodlot on the farm furnished the fuel for heating our home and cooking the food. Staples that needed to be purchased were flour, sugar and salt. Fresh milk arrived from the barn daily and the thick heavy cream rising from it was used for baking and cooking. There still remained a large table in the cellar, which a few years earlier had held numerous milk pans to allow cream to rise daily for sale at the creamery in Plainville. The remaining skim milk was fed to the pigs.

Everyone was busy, although grandmother and grandfather, who died when I was young, spent substantial time reclining, due of the ravages

Robert Bitz with his grandparents William and Lilly Ward. Three generations lived together.

of time. Mother's evenings, the only time she sat down other than when eating, were spent mending clothes. I was really proud when my overalls required their first large patch on the knee, making me look like one of the men. Dad's evening was spent reading the paper, listening to a radio program or going back outside to finish a job before darkness came. His day had started at 5:00 a.m., and Mother's day started shortly after, to provide the family a plentiful hot breakfast to last until dinnertime at noon.

A chemical toilet had arrived by the time I was born. The outhouse, attached to the wood house, still remained but was only used in case of emergency. A cistern that collected rain water from the roof of the house was in the cellar and a pitcher pump brought water from it to a cast iron sink. The water was used for washing hands, cooking and to fill the reservoir on the cast iron kitchen stove, which supplied our hot water. Drinking water came from the well, located between the two houses and dug by my great, great grandfather. We had 'running water' whenever one of us ran back to the house with a full pitcher of water. My dad would often say to me at mealtime, "Bob, go get a pitcher of

water and make sure you get it from the northwest corner of the well."
It was a bit of a joke as he was referring to the fact that our cold weather
storms usually came from the northwest.

The upstairs storeroom and the wood house held kerosene lamps that
were no longer needed since electricity had arrived two years before I
was born. Probably they remained ready to use in case the 'new-fangled'
electricity failed. The modern conveniences, created by electricity,
came slowly. We had a refrigerator, which everyone still called an
icebox, radio, washing machine and incandescent lights throughout the
house. An electric pump and electric water heater didn't arrive until I
was about nine.

We were a close family. My mother had two other unmarried sisters, one
living in Detroit and the other in New York City. They came for a week
at Christmas and spent their summer vacations with us. When they
came home, my sister and I were really spoiled. It was like having three
doting mothers.

Many times I think to myself, "I grew up in the best of times!" It was a
time when I had the opportunity to experience a home life quite similar
to that experienced by many generations before me. It was also a time
when I was able to observe a gradually accelerating change in family
lifestyles. How opportunistic it has been to live at a time when in one's
youth, six miles was a long distance to a time when the moon is now
close, no longer a distant image in the sky!

Hired Men

An integral part of any rural community, during the 1800s and first half of the 1900s, was the hired man. Farming was labor intensive and in most situations the owner of the farm, especially if young sons were not available, needed extra help. Planting and harvest times were especially important. Unless the farmer took advantage of a weather provided window of opportunity there could be significant crop losses. Additionally, a farmer past his prime of life, due to his infirmities, needed help, and a farmer wanting to increase the size of his operation needed additional help.

In my family, my paternal grandfather worked as a hired man for farmers until the later years of his life. When my dad graduated from high school he also worked as a hired man for other farmers.

Perhaps I arrived on earth because my father was a hired man. My maternal grandfather had four daughters and no sons. He had worked with his father on the farm and after his father's death he needed a hired man to accomplish the necessary farm work. Some years later my dad went to work for him and apparently he hit it off well with both my grandfather and my mother. A couple of years later he married my mother and eventually became his father-in-law's partner.

Typically the farmer and hired man made a verbal agreement, beginning April 1 each year, regarding the work required of the hired man, his pay and the other benefits he was to receive. Every few years many hired men looked for greener pastures on another farm, and a movement of hired men would occur on April 1. Some farmers were so demanding that a hired man never stayed a whole year. I'm suspicious that because of my dad's and his father's experiences as hired men, my dad had good long term relationships with his hired men. He learned from first hand experience, "Do unto others as you would have them do unto you."

There were always a few men in every community that, for a variety of reasons, chose not to have a steady job on a farm but were willing to work for a day or a week, when additional help was needed on a farm. Generally these men lived rather frugally and didn't have a telephone. I often accompanied my dad to the general store where the man he was looking for was found sitting on the porch talking with several other men. Dad would then explain his need and hire the man for work the next day. These men worked for several different farmers in the neighborhood as needed and available.

Usually a house was provided on the farm for a married hired man and his family. He was given a plot of land for a garden, four quarts of milk a day, a quarter of beef and a hog once a year in addition to wood for heating his house. The hired man's cash wages were meager and it was

Farm employees enjoying their morning coffee and cookie break circa 1963. Left to right; Chuck Green, Rose Dodge, Charles Pickard, Ida Roth Alice Warner, Harry Bitz, Bob Bitz, Jerry Broekhuizen

seldom possible for him to accumulate enough money to start farming on his own.

Single hired men often boarded with the farm family. If they lived within commuting distance they only had the noon meal with the family. If they lived further away, they were provided a room in the farmer's home and became an extended member of the family. Various times, when I was growing up, my father had a man living with us and one who ate dinner with the family at noon. Dinner was served at noon because farm workers needed a large number of calories to sustain them through the long day.

Hired men, employed by the year, usually did the milking and took care of the livestock. Their day started at five with milking the cows, and then they went home for breakfast. After breakfast the cows were fed, the barns cleaned and afterwards they spent the day working in the fields. An hour was taken for dinner and then it was back to the fields until about four-thirty. Next the cows were milked and their day's work was completed at six. Their work week was seven days but only milking and caring for the livestock was required on Sunday. It was a difficult life but they worked fewer hours than my father who often worked in the evening after supper. Men hired by the day usually worked about eight hours. They started work after the full time men had completed the morning milking and completed their work before the evening milking.

During the 1930s, my dad placed a blind advertisement in the paper for a hired man and received dozens of responses. It was often pitiful to read the responses, which were usually written by the applicant's wife. Times were difficult and people were desperate for work

Over the years our farm had many outstanding employees. One of the men, Charles Green, who my dad hired while I was in high school, worked for us for 40 years. Later his wife and his children also worked many years on our farm. A few years later, when my dad and I were partners, we hired Arthur Kinney who was with us over thirty years until he retired. For a few years Chuck and Art were our only full time employees but as the business grew the number of our employees gradually increased, eventually numbering over 200. The term 'hired man' is no longer appropriate and is now part of the past. Some firms refer to their employees as associates, which is appropriate for both males and females. In our businesses we referred to our fellow workers as "team members." We felt this was the appropriate terminology as we were all working together for similar goals: the production of an outstanding product with a fair return for everyone.

Farm Livestock

Horses and cows were the dominant livestock on our farm. (Turkeys will be discussed in separate chapters.) When turkeys came to the farm chickens were removed, because of possible disease transmission from the chickens to the turkeys.

My dad loved his horses. He had worked with horses since he was a small boy and enjoyed farm horses his entire life. We had two, two-horse teams and a fifth horse that was used for a single horse wagon, for pulling the horse fork or filling out a three-horse hitch when needed. Until we got a tractor in the late 30s, horses did all the heavy farm work.

When I was eight or nine I started driving horses in the hay field and on the horse fork. They were large horses and it was often difficult to put on their harness. Occasionally one stepped on my foot, when I was putting on its harness, and it really hurt! I liked horses but never had great affection for them and was pleased when a tractor arrived on the farm. Dad kept a team of horses until about 1970 and my oldest son Mark had the opportunity to help with them.

We had a small herd of Guernsey cattle, usually milking 10 or 11. They were milked by hand until Dad bought a Surge milking machine around 1943. I was delegated to milk several cows by hand each evening but didn't have to milk in the morning. It wasn't a bad job snuggling up next to the cow, while milking, on a cold winter day but it was a hot job in the summer, especially when the flies were bothering the cows and a tail came flying across my face. I soon learned to put the cow's tail tightly between my calf and thigh to keep the tail from flying into

Four horse team ready to go to work circa 1935

my face. More than once, a cow kicked over the pail of milk or even managed to put its foot into the pail of milk.

The cattle feed attracted mice so we always had a few barn cats. Each time we started milking, they gathered by their dish meowing until they were given some milk. Sometimes, before they were fed, I enjoyed squirting milk from the cow's teat at them to see if they could catch it in their mouth.

From early May to late October the cows were let out to pasture. The pasture extended to a hilly area at the back of the farm. It was often my job in the afternoon to go to the pasture and drive the cows up the lane to the barn. I could go only as fast as the slowest cow moved. If I was in a hurry to get them in the barn to get them milked in time to hear Tom Mix or Jack Armstrong on the radio, I did quite a bit of tail twisting to move them along more rapidly.

The main diet for the cows was hay, or grass if they were on pasture. This was supplemented by a mixture of ground corn, oats and a concentrate with a bit of molasses mixed in to make a tastier treat. This also served as encouragement for the cows to come to the barn. In

Four Guernsey heifers circa 1956. Left to right; Bob Bitz, Chuck Green, Art Kinney, Harry Bitz

the fall and winter, from the time we harvested the potatoes until they were marketed, the cows were given both small and cull potatoes, that were chopped so they wouldn't choke on a large potato in their throat. In the early spring we drew pea ensilage (pea vines) from the vinery, two miles north of the farm, where we had marketed our pea crop the previous summer. The cows relished the pea vines even though they had a powerful offensive odor.

Each evening the milk pails and strainer were rinsed with cold water and left in a small addition to the barn called the milk house. Each morning Dad took them to the house where mother washed them with soap and hot water. The evening milking was put in 10 gallon cans and placed in refrigerated water to cool. A few years earlier, before electricity, my dad had cut ice on the nearby river and stored it in the icehouse to use for cooling the milk during the remainder of the year. The morning milk went directly in the can and out to the milk stand next to the highway to be picked up by the milk truck each morning.

The milk truck took the milk to Syracuse and returned the empty cans in the afternoon, seven days a week, 365 days a year.

I learned about the birds and the bees at an early age because of the cows. My dad kept a bull that had an ugly disposition, something that Guernsey bulls are noted for. It bellowed and pawed at the floor in its pen encouraging me to pass by as quickly as I could. One Sunday morning a cow was in heat so dad put a rope in the bull's nose and led the bull to the barnyard to breed the cow. The bull performed his duty but when dad started leading the bull back to the barn the bull suddenly attacked him and was quickly rolling dad around in the mud of the barnyard. I ran into the barn, grabbed a pitch fork and rammed it into the bull's rear end. The bull was immediately distracted and I quickly got out of the way. This gave dad time to get up and away from the bull. The next morning the bull got a ride to the slaughterhouse and soon artificial insemination came to the farm.

Harry Bitz cultivating his garden circa 1950.

Harry Bitz and Robert Bitz with wagon waiting for a hired combine to unload its grain into wagon circa 1937. The farm buildings in the background belonged to Oscar and Ernest Fletcher. Harry Bitz purchased their farm about five years later.

Dad liked pigs although there hadn't been any on the farm for several years. When I was about 12 he said, "Bob how would you like to grow some pigs?" I fell in with the idea and we went to a farm and bought three young pigs (shoats). I took care of them morning and night. In the winter we butchered two for home consumption and took the third to a neighbor who had a boar. The two of them became quite friendly. A little less than four months later she produced 10 healthy baby pigs. I enjoyed taking care of them and my dad said I could have whatever money we could get from them at market time. I had a windfall! It was during World War II and meat was both scarce and high priced. I put the money into war bonds and the money came in handy 10 years later. My pig raising experience was so enjoyable I had each of my boys raise some pigs when they were about 12, but they didn't receive the high prices that I did.

Hay

Hay is essential for horses and cows during late fall, winter and early spring when there is no pasture available. Grass seed was sown in combination with wheat in the fall, and a legume was seeded on top of the same field in late winter. The freezing and thawing of the ground, during late winter, helped cover the legume seed with soil. After the wheat was harvested in July, the grass and legume established a good root system and a crop of hay could be harvested the following June. It is an example of the need for farmers not to think in terms of days, weeks or months, but in years to ensure they had the necessary feed for their livestock.

Fortunately the days of mowing with the scythe had ended long before I arrived. Hay was cut with a five foot wide mowing machine, pulled by a team of horses, and raked into windrows after the hay had partially dried. We always tried to mow the hay when the sky looked like it wouldn't rain for two or three days because if the hay got wet it's quality decreased and it made extra work trying to get the hay dry again. It was always a struggle to get the hay dry and in the barn before it rained.

A team of horses was hitched to a wagon with a hay loader fastened behind. My job was to drive the horses while dad positioned the hay in layers evenly over the wagon. I started out standing on the wagon and as the size of the load increased I gradually moved up the ladder to keep from being buried in the hay. The ladder, which was the width of the wagon, was mainly to keep hay from falling off the front of the wagon. Occasionally a misdirected fork full of hay would land on top of my head but it was something that I learned to ignore.

Circa 1930 photo of a wagon and hay loader.

When the wagon was fully loaded, the hay loader was unhitched from the back of the wagon, and we headed to the barn to transfer the hay into the barn's mow. The horses dug in their hooves and pulled mightily to bring the wagon up the barn bridge and on to the barn floor. Only a single board stood between the horses and the barnyard 10 feet below. Apparently they knew enough to watch out for their own safety because I never heard of a team taking the plunge.

Another horse was brought from the barn to furnish the power to lift the hay to the top of the barn. A rope, that ran to the top of the barn and down to a large grapple fork on the wagon, was connected to a whiffletree behind the horse. When the grapple fork was set, my dad told me to start the horse and the horse pulled the hay to the top of the barn and then along a track to the appropriate spot in the mow. It was important to stop the horse immediately, when I was instructed to, or the hay ended up in the wrong spot and I got blamed. It was very hot and hard work in the hay mow. The man working in the mow always became drenched with sweat and if the hay ended up where it was more difficult to mow, it was not looked upon kindly.

There was a chute, about three feet square with a ladder on one side, extending from the basement to the top of the barn. In the fall, when it came time to feed hay to the livestock, a man climbed the chute to the top of the mow and threw enough hay down to the animals to last a day. A 'rule of thumb' was that half of the hay should be remaining on Groundhog's Day (February 2) to have enough for the livestock until they were put on pasture in May.

About 1947, dad bought a pickup baler and the days of handling loose hay ended. Mowing away bales of hay was still a hot job but it was better than handling loose hay. Haying was still hard work when I was a young man but far easier than in the days of my great grandfather when it was cut with a scythe, raked into piles, pitched onto a wagon and pitched from the wagon into the hay mow, all by hand. The number of hours spent harvesting a ton of hay was far greater in those days!

Wheat and Oats

Wheat has been a cash crop for Central New York farmers from the time the area was first settled. It continued to be a cash crop on most farms into the 1950s but on our farm it was fed to the turkeys. Oats were raised as feed for both horses and cows but also made a good feed for turkeys.

Both wheat and oats are considered small grains and are sown with a grain drill. Wheat was planted about the middle of September and oats in April, when the ground was sufficiently dry in the spring. Wheat was harvested in July and oats in August, both with a grain binder. The grain binder was a huge improvement over the grain cradle that was used a century earlier.

After the field had been prepared for planting, a team of horses was fastened to a grain drill, the wheat or oats were put into the drill's grain box and fertilizer dumped into the grain drill's fertilizer box. The man planting the grain and driving the horses walked behind the grain drill. If the ground was dry and the weather warm, a man that was white when he started the day, ended the day a dirty brown. Drilling grain wasn't considered hard work but it was tiring, walking behind the grain drill on loose dirt hours at a time. A good farmer took pride in how straight he could drive the horses across the field and his capabilities were quietly judged by neighboring farmers as they drove past.

Grain harvest was a busy time on a farm. It had to be harvested when it was almost ripe and when the weather cooperated. When I was a boy we had a grain binder, pulled by three horses, that both cut and bound the grain into bundles. Dad drove the grain binder and the hired men set the bundles up into shocks to dry for a few days, before they were hauled to the barn. After dad purchased a tractor in 1939, I was designated to ride on the binder, manipulating the various levers and dropping the bundles in rows, while he drove the tractor.

The grain was cut before it was completely dry, when the kernels of grain were still held tightly in the grain heads and did not fall to the ground. We always hoped that it wouldn't rain during the few days the grain was drying in the shocks, as rain delayed the process and made extra work.

The same wagon that was used to draw hay to the barn was used for the grain. One man used a pitch fork to throw the bundles on the wagon while another man piled the bundles neatly on the wagon with grain heads pointed to the inside and the butts to the outside. This had to be carefully done to keep the grain from falling off the wagon on the way to the barn. At the barn, the bundles of grain were either pitched into the mow or a grapple horse fork was used to take a number of bundles

Circa 1930 photo of pitching bundles of wheat on a wagon.

A photo taken in 1938 on the farm (now owned by Mark Bitz) at the top of Jaycox Hill. Bundles of grain are being drawn to the threshing machine and the straw is being baled by a stationery baler. Bob Bitz and Olin Hudson are on top of the threshing machine.

at one time. The man in the mow layered the bundles evenly over the mow so they could be removed easily when it was time for threshing.

Threshing day was one of the busiest days on the farm. A century earlier, a farmer used a flail to remove the grain from the stalks, and he spent many fall and winter days in the process. The threshing machine was much faster but required a large crew. Few farmers could afford to have a threshing machine of their own so they hired a man with a tractor and threshing machine to do custom work on their farm.

The threshing machine owner backed the machine onto our barn floor and connected a long endless belt from a pulley on the thresher to the pulley on his large tractor to furnish the necessary power. He fed the grain bundles into the thresher as two or three men pitched the bundles from the mow to his threshing platform. Another two men were

Circa 1930 photo of William Ward on a grain binder.

required to carry the threshed grain into the granary for storage and two men were needed to form the straw into a stack in the barnyard. An additional person was needed to operate the straw blower on the threshing machine to place it where the men forming the stack needed it at any particular time. All of this work took a minimum of eight men but usually there were about ten. None of the farmers had enough help available so two or three neighbors exchanged work and one or two men were hired as day labor.

It was hot dusty work for all the crew but the two men forming the straw stack had the dirtiest job. Dust and chaff were blowing at these sweaty men all day. They usually tied a large handkerchief around their head and over their nose to keep some of the dust from entering their lungs. It was not uncommon for a man to ache with dust poisoning for a day or two after threshing.

Mother had been busy the previous day as well as threshing day, preparing food for the threshers. Mashed potatoes, gravy, platters of meat and apple pie with cheese were staples for the threshers' dinner. A bench with wash basins, soap and warm water was set up outside the kitchen for the men to clean up before they came in for dinner. It was a jolly time at the dinner table, while the men were eating, as they joked with each other while filling their empty stomachs. The man with the threshing machine had dinner on many different farms, most of which he looked forward to but occasionally one that he dreaded.

On our farm, threshing was done two different times. Wheat was threshed in early August and oats threshed about two weeks later. If it was possible, dad had the thresher set up his machine in the oat field so he could draw the bundles of oats directly from the shocks to the threshing machine. The grain was put into bags, which were tied and then drawn to the barn. A custom baler was hired to come to the farm and bale the straw. Whenever this could be done it saved work but depended upon the availability of the threshing machine. I remember once when threshing oats and baling straw were being accomplished in a field at the same time.

Circa 1937 photo of a hired combine cutting grain adjacent to turkey brooding buildings.

One of dad's wagons was made from the heavy frame of a Pierce-Arrow automobile. When the thresher checked to see how many bushels of oats the threshing machine recorded for that load, there were over 100 bushels on the wagon. It was a huge load for the team of horses pulling the wagon, straw and 3,200 pounds of oats. The same day a friend and I bagged and tied over 1,000 bushels of oats. We were both tired that night!

About 1948, an Allis Chalmers combine with a grain bagging attachment was purchased and the days of the large threshing crew ended. Now it only took two men to harvest and thresh the grain in the same amount of time that it had earlier taken to form the grain into bundles. This was just one step of many I have seen in the development of efficiency on our farms.

Although my story is related to farming when I was a young boy in the 1930s and 40s, a brief review of the changes since then, on our farm, in our oat and wheat harvest, are appropriate. The next advancement was an Allis Chalmers combine with a bin followed by a Massy Harris self-propelled combine with a 12 foot cut and without a cab. The next combine was larger and had a cab to protect the operator from the dust. Gradually our combines got larger and larger, with air conditioning and grain heads 30 feet wide. Now one man can plant and harvest as much grain in the same amount of time as it would have taken several hundred men, 200 years ago. The tremendous efficiency of American agriculture has substantially raised the standard of living for everyone.

Corn

Corn was grown on our farm in the 1930s, similarly to the way it had been grown for the previous 200 years. The only major difference was that a simple hand operated corn planter was used instead of dropping the seeds from the fingers. Low yielding Indian flint corn was grown, and a one row horse pulled cultivator, followed by hand hoeing, controlled the weeds. Each hill of corn was individually cut with a hand held corn knife, shaped like a sickle. The corn cut from about 40 hills was leaned vertically against each other to form a shock. Binder twine was tied around the shock to hold it together and prevent strong winds from blowing it over. The shocks of corn resembled the Native American tepees and formed picturesque fall scenes in many old-time farm paintings, that had pumpkins interspersed among them.

The corn was cut before the ears and stalks were dry allowing the drying to finish in the shocks. During the late fall and winter the shocks were dismantled and the ears of corn husked and stored in a corn crib or

Shocking corn to the south of the brick house on Jaycox Hill circa 1914.

A field of corn shocks drying in a field. The corn ears will be husked during the winter and the stalks fed to cattle.

immediately shelled as feed for the farm's livestock. The stalks were hauled to the barn and fed to the cows. The parts of the stalks that the cows didn't eat were thrown into the barnyard and later drawn to the fields, along with straw and animal waste, to provide fertilizer for the next crop grown.

As the 30s progressed, gradual changes were made in our farm's methods for growing corn. A two row planter came first, followed by a silo in 1939 when the first tractor was purchased. Silo corn was now cut with a corn binder, somewhat similar to a grain binder but designed for the much larger stalks of corn. The corn bundles were pitched on a wagon and hauled to an ensilage cutter, powered by the tractor, and chopped into small pieces to be blown into the silo. Grain corn was husked directly from the standing corn stalks in the field and drawn to the corn crib. About 1941, Paul Huntington, a nearby young farmer who had purchased a corn picker, was hired to pick the few acres of husking corn that dad grew.

As our farm acres increased and more corn was grown, a single row corn picker became part of the farm's equipment, additional corn cribs came into use and a tractor powered corn sheller was purchased. Soon a piece of wonderful new technology came into use, especially since I felt half

On the left is a hand operated corn planter used from the late 1800s until the 1930s. It was a big advancement over dropping the corn kernels by hand into corn hills. On the right is a dibble to make holes in the ground for tobacco or cabbage plants. This type of tool was used by farmers for centuries.

A photo of two corn shellers. The one on the left was used from the late 1800s to the middle 1900s. The one on the right was used during the early 1800s.

of my summer was spent hoeing and pulling weeds. 2-4-D, a chemical that killed broadleaf weeds, eliminated the dreaded tasks of hoeing and pulling weeds. It was relatively inexpensive and was easily sprayed on both corn and weeds, without hurting the corn. It also eliminated the need to cultivate the corn.

When I came back to the farm from Cornell, we started increasing the number of turkeys we grew and needed more corn. The new equipment and improved technology permitted more and more corn to be grown without increasing the necessary labor. Two time consuming and relatively difficult tasks involved in corn production remained. The ears of corn had to be put in corn cribs to dry and later shelled for use as turkey feed. When corn headers were made for grain combines and grain dryers came into use in the 1950s, all phases of corn production became mechanized.

Corn breeders have made tremendous improvements in corn yields. Hybrid corns with improved yields came into common use in the 1930s and, since then, corn breeders have gradually improved yields. There are varieties of corn bred for optimum production in both long and short season climates, varieties that are resistant to pests and ones that are bred for dryer climates.

As I write this in 2012, I would estimate that a farmer can grow and harvest an acre of corn while spending less than two hours in the total process, compared with 100 hours it would have taken for my great grandfather to accomplish the same task. In addition the average corn yield per acre today is about eight times as large as it was in the early 1800s, making an increase in production per hour of approximately 400 times! This becomes extremely significant to me because I have seen most of that change during my lifetime.

Potatoes

Potatoes were a cash crop on our farm from the late 1800s until 1952. The rapidly increasing population of Syracuse provided a strong market. Improved roads made it possible for the 40 mile round-trip to the Syracuse Public Market to be completed in a day. Because of hills and dirt roads, 30 bushels of potatoes was the maximum load the horses could pull. Trips to the market were limited to days in the fall when roads were dry, and on mild winter days when packed snow permitted transport on a set of bobs. (Bobs are similar to a wagon except they have a runner placed where each of the wheels are on a wagon.) Grandfather left home at 11:00 p.m. and returned about 4:00 p.m. the next day. If he was fortunate to receive 60 cents a bushel, he returned at the end of his 17 hour trip with $18 to pay for the cost of growing and marketing the potatoes.

In the 1930s, almost all of our farm neighbors grew two to ten acres of potatoes and marketed them on the Syracuse public market or to potato dealers. An additional bonus of growing potatoes was they were the largest source of calories for almost every farm family and needed to be grown even if none were sold. My dad grew six acres and sold them on the Syracuse market as well as to dealers. Grandfather bought a truck in about 1917, which was only usable when roads were dry but with concrete roads a few years later it took less than an hour to reach Syracuse. The truck was small and at times he also drew potatoes to the market with horses. Often in the fall, a customer would buy 10 or 15 bushel if we were willing to deliver them to the potato bin in their cellar. It was good exercise carrying the potatoes down steep, narrow cellar stairs and depositing them in the potato bin.

Potatoes being harvested. Until about 1940 the potato digger was pulled by three horses rather than a tractor. Two people working together picked up the potatoes and put them in crates. The crates of potatoes were transported to the barn and dumped in the potato storage for later grading and sale. The empty crates were returned to the field to be filled with potatoes again.

In 1907, grandfather built a new barn with one quarter of the basement designed for storing potatoes. We drove the horses and wagon onto the barn floor and dumped the potatoes through doors in the floor making large piles of potatoes in the cellar below. Many wet fall and cold winter days were spent in the potato cellar sorting potatoes and bagging them for market. Dad kept a portable kerosene stove in the basement to prevent the potatoes from freezing on especially cold days during the winter.

A one row potato planter pulled by a team of horses was used for planting. One person drove the horses while another person made sure the seed potatoes were evenly spaced for dropping in the ground and being covered with dirt. Before planting, Dad cut each potato into several pieces, making sure there was an eye on each one, to permit its growth when planted. For cutting the seed, he had an extremely thin knife that sliced easily through the potato.

Planting was followed by cultivating, hilling and weeding. The potatoes had to be sprayed frequently to control potato bugs that ate the vines. The sprayer was drawn by horses and powered by gears from one of the wheels. Wearing no special protection, the operator was usually covered with the chemicals from the spray. It was a dangerous job but the danger went unrecognized. In the 1940s, a man in the community purchased a tractor with mounted spray tanks. He formed a spray circle and contracted with dozens of farmers to spray their potatoes. Most of the farmers were pleased to have this service, which relieved them of a dirty job. Unfortunately, some years later the operator of the spray ring died of cancer.

Potatoes were dug in late September or early October. A one row potato digger was pulled by horses and people followed behind, picking the potatoes from the ground and putting them in bushel crates. Two years, during World War II, German prisoners-of- war helped harvest the potatoes. One year, when prisoners weren't available, I stayed out of school a week to help pick up the potatoes. It was a long week!

By 1952, specialization was reaching the farm and we discontinued growing potatoes. We decided to move toward turkey production and eliminated potatoes as part of the farm operation.

Tobacco

It is ironical that my family raised tobacco for over 80 years, yet none of us ever used any. Perhaps seeing and smelling it was enough for them to wonder how anyone could smoke or chew tobacco. The fact that it provided, for many years, more profit than any other farm crop was a strong incentive to grow tobacco. Another reason was that the climate and soils, where our farm was located, provided consistently good crops.

Tobacco was an extremely labor intensive crop and timeliness each step of the way from planting to marketing were critical for success. The tiny tobacco seeds were planted in a sandy spot in May, transplanted in late June, harvested in September, processed during the winter and finally marketed in February. It was a long process and the farmer wasn't paid for any of the crop until it was marketed. Occasionally the entire crop could be lost to only a minute of violent hail during the month before harvest.

In the little hamlet of Plainville there were three tobacco warehouses with sorting rooms and cigar production. In Baldwinsville there were several large tobacco warehouses and cigar makers. Hundreds of people, in addition to farmers, found employment in the tobacco industry in and around Syracuse.

When tobacco was first grown in the Baldwinsville area about 1850, there were few other opportunities for a farmer to grow a crop that gave a good return. Wheat had been the dominant cash crop until an insect called the wheat midge attacked farmers' wheat crops in 1845. There was little opportunity for much income from dairying as this was before cheese factories and creameries came into existence and when

A lithograph of the William Wilson tobacco farm in 1878. All of the buildings are gone except for the upright part of the house.

most farms milked only two or three cows. Even though it was necessary to build a special barn for drying tobacco, the opportunities tobacco presented were attractive.

Production on our farm never exceeded four acres, partially because of the cost of building drying barns, called tobacco sheds, and partially because of the tremendous amount of labor required. Our farm, like most farms, grew a variety of crops as a type of insurance so if one crop failed the others might provide enough income to keep the farm operating another year. Only a portion of the farm's land was suitable for tobacco and not more than a quarter of that land could be used any year. Tobacco drew many nutrients from the soil making it unwise to grow it on the same ground more than one year out of four.

A neighboring farm, that my father purchased in 1952, had a thriving tobacco business during the last half of the 1800s. William Wilson, the owner, was the grandson of the first Plainville settler. Cuba was the

A view of some of the buildings on the William Wilson farm taken 64 years after the lithograph.

center of tobacco production in the Americas and was known for its high quality tobacco. Mr. Wilson went to Cuba to observe their tobacco production and obtain seeds but was prohibited from taking seed out of the country. He then wrote a letter home and, with an adhesive, attached a number of the tiny seeds to the paper in the letter. Upon arrival back in Plainville, he planted the seeds and was able to produce tobacco superior to what had been grown. In 1879 he sold seed from this tobacco for $3 an ounce, a much higher price than the ordinary seed but it produced both more and higher quality tobacco. Mr. Wilson also set up a cigar manufacturing business on his farm and became one of the most successful farmers in the area.

Once tobacco has been transplanted, it requires cultivating and hoeing several times during the growing period to remove weeds that would diminish yield. Tobacco worms appeared soon after the plants had been transplanted and it was necessary to walk through the field, row by row, searching for the little worms. When you found one it was squashed between your fingers, ending its tobacco eating days. They had voracious appetites and consumed the tender leaves. Tobacco buyers paid less for tobacco with holes in the leaves and the leaves weighed less with holes in them. Occasionally a worm was missed and on the next trip through the field it would be large enough to throw against a stone and make a big splat! Both George Washington and Thomas Jefferson used turkeys in their tobacco fields to eat worms on the plants.

In August it was necessary to break off the top of each plant to prevent the plant from expending its energy growing unwanted seeds, rather than the desired leaves. The tobacco

Wilson's Hybrid Havana Tobacco Seed.

SAME AS GROWN IN 1876, AND TRUE TO NAME.

Originated by

◁WM. WILSON & SON,▷

Plainville, Onondaga County, New York.

Our Seed is acknowledged by all Manufacturers and Dealers as the Best Havana Seed Tobacco known to the trade.

Profitable to the Growers, and desired by the Manufacturers.

As Blood will tell in the animal kingdom, so Pure Seed will tell in the Vegetable.

Be sure you are right, then go ahead. None Genuine unless put up in packages bearing our Trade Mark (A Tobacco Seed Plant) on one side and directions for Sowing, Growing, and Handling on the other.

Don't be imposed upon, nor sow any but the Genuine Seed. Price, $1 per oz.

WM. WILSON & SON, Originators,
[OVER.]   Plainville, Onondaga Co., N.Y.

An advertising sheet for William Wilson's tobacco seed, originally from Cuba, that he sold in 1879 for $3 an ounce.

plant refused to give up its urge to produce seed and after topping started forming suckers, to grow into seed producers. To control this, the suckers were broken off after they had grown a few inches and the plant's energy was again directed toward making larger leaves.

Before harvest, tobacco buyers representing large tobacco companies came to look at the crop and make offers for its purchase. During the time I remember, there was seldom much competition. In about 1942, I remember my dad coming in the house, shaking his head in astonishment, and telling the unbelievably high offer the buyer had made for his tobacco; more than double the usual price. This was most unusual as the grower was usually at the mercy of the buyers. One year, a well to do farmer in Plainville refused to sell his crop because the offers were so low, however that was an unusual situation.

At harvest time each tobacco stalk was cut near the ground and left to lie in the sun for a short time to wilt, making it less likely to lose leaves when handled. Next the stalks were put into small piles and then individually pierced near the butt with a sharp tobacco spud to slide six

Three farmers setting tobacco plants circa 1900. Tobacco setters were manufactured in nearby Memphis in the late 1800s.

A circa 1920 photo of farmers harvesting tobacco.

A farmer drawing harvested tobacco to the tobacco shed on a tobacco rack.

or seven plants on to a four foot long wooden lath. The laths of tobacco were hung on a special wagon rack and hauled to the tobacco shed to be hung on tobacco hangers for drying. Several men were required to pass each lath with tobacco from one to the other to first fill the very top of the barn. Each lath was placed about six inches from the last to allow air to pass between the plants and gradually dry the tobacco during the next two or three months. The tobacco sheds had long vertical narrow doors that could be opened or closed to allow the proper amount of air to enter the barn.

On a foggy November or December day the tobacco, still on the lath, was removed from the hangers in the barn and put in piles next to an enclosed room in the tobacco shed, called a stripping room. A stove, with a large open container of water on top, produced steam in the

Hanging lathes of tobacco in a tobacco shed to dry during the fall months. Three or four men passed the lathes, one to another, up to the top of the barn.

stripping room to keep the tobacco leaves from being dry and brittle. The leaves were pulled from the stalks and put, butt end out, in paper lined wooden boxes and pressed into tight bundles. Each bundle weighed about 30 pounds. The bundles were then stored until it was time to deliver the tobacco to the buyer.

During the late 1800s, on the day specified for delivery, long lines of farmers with their tobacco loaded on wagons pulled by horses waited in turn to unload their tobacco and receive their checks for the year's work. That was a happy day, not only for the farmers but also the area merchants.

Because of the shortage of labor on farms during World War II, many area farmers discontinued producing tobacco. A few continued to

The cigar manufacturing building on the William Wilson farm. This photo was taken in 1952 after the building had sat idle for many years.

grow tobacco into the 1950s but soon all tobacco production ended in Central New York. As a person drives along the country roads in Lysander and Van Buren today, occasionally a tobacco shed remains, a remnant of 100 years ago when the tobacco industry was a major economic driver in Central New York.

Peas & Beans

About 1930, a pea vinery was constructed two miles north of our farm and provided area farmers another choice for a cash crop. The vinery had four open sides and a roof to cover the pea shelling equipment. The vines, after the peas had been removed, were elevated to an outside stack and the shelled peas were put in bulk containers and hauled to a processing plant for canning. It was a simple operation, located near many farmers, permitting those without a truck to draw peas to the vinery with horses and wagon. The pea season was short, lasting only from late June to the middle of July.

During the latter part of the following winter farmers, who had delivered peas to the vinery, were permitted to load vines from the pea vine stack to feed to their cows. The vines, which had a powerful stench, were pitched on to a wagon or truck and then pitched off to feed the cows. Even though we thought the vines smelled bad, the cows went after them like a boy eating candy.

The peas were planted as soon as the ground was dry enough to be worked in the spring. A representative from the pea vinery stopped, almost daily, when they were about ready to be harvested. When the representative determined they were ready, the farmer was given a specific day for harvest, regardless of weather, holiday or other plans the farmer had. My dad always thought they had him harvest the peas too soon because at maturity the size of the peas and their weight increased daily, providing a larger payment check.

The peas were cut with the same mowing machine that was used to cut the hay. The pea vines lay flat on the ground and were difficult to cut without plugging the mowing machine. This made it necessary for a man, other than the one driving the horses pulling the mower, to walk along behind, and use a pitch fork to continually pull vines from the mower to keep it from plugging. After mowing, a pitchfork was used to put the vines in small piles and then the piles were pitched on a truck or wagon to take to the vinery where they were pitched off for shelling. The pea vinery was a fun place for a boy who enjoyed using a small piece of pipe for a pea shooter. My friend, Olin Hudson, and I had great pleasure in pelting each other with large ripe peas.

There was a great deal of hard work involved in growing peas, and the farmer never knew if the weather would smile on him and provide a good crop. Prices for farm crops were low in the 1930s and farmers had a hard time surviving through that difficult period. Pea vineries gradually went out of business in Central NY during the 1940s as production increased in other parts of the country and as pea harvesters were developed that shelled the peas from the standing vines.

Red Kidney Beans

About 1940, when Dad began to farm more acres, he started growing red kidney beans. They were planted with a corn planter and because he could hire someone to thresh them in the fall, the only extra equipment needed was a relatively simple bean puller. The bean puller had two wide knives that didn't cut the roots but cut into the top of the ground and pulled two rows of beans at a time.

Growing beans was not especially labor intensive except at harvest time when they were put into piles with a pitchfork. They needed several days of sunshine to dry sufficiently for threshing. The cloudy and rainy days, south of Lake Ontario in the fall, often made threshing a challenge. Usually it rained before they were threshed, making it necessary to turn the piles with a fork to dry out after a rain. This might happen several times. Often it was necessary to wait a few days for the threshing machine, when it was busy threshing other farmers' beans. Rain coming in the meantime, required another drying period.

When the bean combine arrived, the beans were pitched into it as it moved across the field from pile to pile. The dust flew, making another dirty job for the farmer. Eventually Dad bought a combine, which made bean harvest much easier. He continued to grow beans into the middle 1950s when bean production was discontinued as we put increased emphasis on turkey production.

Cabbage

L arge rubber boots on his feet, a rake in his hand and a chew of tobacco in his mouth were the essentials for the man in the sliced cabbage pit at the local sauerkraut factory. What did the man do when he finished his chew or had to spit? Did he swallow it? Heads of cabbage traveled on a conveyer to where a worker removed the tough core and then the heads passed through a slicing machine on to a wheelbarrow to be wheeled down an alleyway to the pit where the man was leveling the cabbage. As I waited to unload my truckload of cabbage I had the opportunity to observe the inter workings of the transformation of large heads of cabbage into one of a German's favorite foods.

Five months earlier the life of the head of cabbage began in bed. No, not a bed similar to one we lie in but in a plot of sandy well-prepared ground. Thousands and thousands of tiny cabbage seeds were distributed evenly and covered with a thin layer of soil, which now became a cabbage bed. The bed was regularly watered to keep the cabbage seeds moist while the warm energy from the sun and the nutrients (fertilizer) added to the soil provided the essential elements for the seeds to germinate and develop into small cabbage plants.

Any weeds that developed from unwanted seeds that had been sitting silently in the soil, waiting for the right opportunity to grow, were pulled by hand. When the cabbage plants were about five inches high it was time for them to be removed from their bed. A five tined fork was used to loosen the ground so the plants could easily be removed from the bed.

A transplanter, pulled by a team of horses, and operated by a three-person team placed the cabbage plants in three-foot rows with the plants spaced 10 inches apart. One person drove the horses and two

Harry Bitz and Chuck Green pitching heads of cabbage from a wagon to a truck prior to delivery at a sauerkraut factory. Circa 1950

people alternatively placed a cabbage plant in a soil opening made by the planter. Every 12 inches the planter would click and a cup of water would flow from a barrel of water on the planter. The water engulfed the plant's roots and surrounding soil, ensuring the plant would have moisture for a healthy start. A team of horses that moved at a slow steady pace was essential to having the plants spaced exactly at the time the water dropped on their roots. A fly on the nose or a mosquito on the back of the people setting the plants had to be ignored. There was no time for distractions!

Every week or two, after setting the cabbage plants, it was necessary to carefully cultivate and hoe the field to prevent weeds from developing. Weeds removed moisture and nutrients from the soil that were needed by the cabbage plants to develop into large heads. It was also necessary to spray the plants to prevent cabbageworms from damaging the crop.

By September the cabbage was ready to be harvested. We used large butcher knives to cut the heads from the cabbage plant roots. It was backbreaking work, bending over one plant after another, cutting first one head, then the next and tossing them between the rows, to later be thrown on to the truck that hauled them to the sauerkraut factory. Some sauerkraut factories required that the heads be thrown on and off the truck by hand. This was hard work and time consuming. We preferred the factories that allowed us to use a pitchfork since we could handle two heads at a time and didn't have to bend over for each head. Even that was difficult as many of the heads weighed more than 10 pounds each. The natural fertilizer, produced by the turkeys, had done its work well. Some of the heads weighed close to 20 pounds! Usually our cabbage went to the sauerkraut factory in Clay but at times we hauled it to the 'Sauerkraut Capital of NY' at Phelps, about 50 miles away. Cabbage was another crop we discontinued growing in the 1950s.

The ride home from the sauerkraut factory provided a short rest and gave me time to ponder whether the man in the sauerkraut pit swallowed or spit. I never found out for sure but I think I know the answer!

The Farm Woodlot

The heat that comes from burning wood, to keep the house warm, is the last of multiple heatings the wood provides. Each step of the way, from woodlot to kitchen stove, has warmed the ones making it happen!

Often, on a cold winter day, my dad would announce that we were going to work in the woods that day. It might be near zero with a cold wind, that would make many people stay inside to keep warm, but if you were cutting wood, there was no need for artificial warmth.

A team of horses was hooked to the bobs, then axes, crosscut saw, beetle, wedges and log chains were loaded on the bobs before heading to the woods. It was cold, until we had penetrated a hundred yards into the woods, and then, suddenly the wind disappeared. There was a stillness in the air, punctuated by our voices and then by the teeth of the crosscut saw making the undercut in the base of the tree chosen for harvesting. Next loud sounds of an axe reverberated through the woods as blows from the axe notched the undercut on the side of the tree in the direction it was to fall. With the crosscut saw in the hands of two men a rhythm developed as the saw ate through the wood. Soon there was a loud crash as this giant of nature crashed to the ground.

By this time, coats had been removed and small branches on the tree were removed with an axe. Next, the crosscut was used to cut the trunk and large branches into manageable four feet lengths. Since the pieces near the trunk were still too heavy to lift, the beetle and wedges were used to split them into four foot lengths that one man could manage.

As noontime approached, the bobs were piled high with wood and men and horses headed to the farmstead. The lengths of wood were stacked near the house to await being cut into one foot lengths by the buzz saw, later some winter day. The horses were put in the barn and given a measure of oats and some hay while the men replenished their bodies with a hearty meal at the dinner table before heading back to the woodlot. When evening came there was no need for a treadmill or other exercise as a means to sleep soundly. Thousands of calories had been burned in this first step in obtaining fuel for next winter's fires.

At a later date, when the stack of wood had reached a sufficient size, the pulley on the buzz saw was connected to the pulley on the tractor, which furnished the power to cut the longer lengths of wood into shorter stove-length pieces. Perhaps you have heard a carpenter's small electric saw cutting through a piece of wood. The buzz saw blade was many times larger and made a much louder, longer lasting sound as it chewed its way through a large chunk of wood.

The chunks that needed splitting were thrown into a large pile and the next job, whenever time became available, was to split the chunks into smaller pieces that would fit into the kitchen stove to provide the necessary heat for cooking and baking. An axe was used to split the chunks and this process, like the others, generated a great deal of heat for the person doing the splitting.

The split wood sat outside in a large pile, gradually drying as the warm summer sun shone upon it. On a warm August day a wagon was loaded with some of the wood, which was hauled to the woodshed, attached to the kitchen of the house. As a young boy I was drafted to help with this chore and carried wood from the wagon to the woodshed where my dad stacked it into neat rows. Neat stacks were necessary to have a sufficient supply of wood for the winter and keep the piles from leaning and falling on someone when the wood was removed. As I got older and gained experience I was delegated to haul and pile the wood. Yes, even this part of the process provided plenty of heat!

Harry Bitz drawing a sled full of wood to the rear part of the brick house on Jaycox Hill circa 1920.

The last step in the process of moving the wood from the wood house to the kitchen was the only one that didn't generate much heat. Daily, from fall to spring, I had the chore of keeping the woodbox, resting between the woodshed and kitchen, full. This only took a few minutes each day. There was no heat in the woodshed.

Less energy was needed to prepare wood to be burned in the furnace of the house, as large chunks were needed for fall and spring. This eliminated the splitting of that wood. Even less energy was required when a tree trunk was cut into lengths of eight to sixteen feet for logs to be sawed into lumber.

Dad had a log boat, that he used to haul logs out of the wood lot. One end of a chain was fastened to the side of the log boat, which was turned on its side and positioned next to the log. Then the chain was placed under one end of the log and back over the top of the log boat. By hooking the horses to the loose end of the chain and having them pull it only a few feet the log boat righted itself with the log landing on top. The horses could then haul the log to a nearby sawmill.

We never cut large quantities of trees for logs, but just what was needed for small projects. A variety of lumber was kept in the barn to have available for what might be needed during the year. The wood lot was less than 10 acres but supplied the necessary firewood for two families on the farm for over a century. A wood lot is like any other crop on the farm except it is managed and harvested in terms of decades rather than months.

The chain saw came into common use during the 1940s and replaced the crosscut saw. Cutting wood for fuel was still hard work but became much easier with the gasoline powered chain saw cutting its way through the tree as easily as a knife cutting through butter. In the 1960s we changed our source of heating fuel from wood to oil. The days of home grown heat for the houses and several sessions of heat produced by the body in changing trees into firewood were gone but still bring warm memories.

Fencing

When fencing on the farm, we didn't use foils and it wasn't dangerous but it did involve substantial effort every spring and early summer. Unless livestock is confined to a building, a fence around their pasture is necessary to keep them from wandering and getting into trouble.

Our farm, like most others in Central New York, had some land that was too hilly or too wet to plow and plant crops, so a fence was built around its perimeter and it became permanent pasture for cattle and horses. These fences were made of several strands of barbed wire stapled to wooden posts spaced about a rod (16 1/2 feet) apart.

Every spring, a roll of barbed wire, fence posts, 16 pound maul, hammer, pliers, fence stretcher and staples were loaded on a wagon and a circuit was made along the perimeter of the pasture. Winter snows in our area average over 100 inches. In protected areas, drifting snow was well above the fence and as the snow settled, it exerted significant pressure on the strands of barbed wire. The weight of the snow sometimes pulled the staples or broke the wire leaving a fence that invited the livestock to explore what was on the other side. As a result the fence had to be repaired before the livestock could be turned out to pasture in the spring.

Although we tried to keep our fences in good repair, I remember several instances of someone stopping by our house at night and yelling, "Your cows are out!" This required our family to immediately put on our clothes, grab flashlights and attempt to find the cows and return them to the pasture. Since it was almost hopeless to find where they had made their escape in the dark, we confined them to the barnyard until we

A photo of a stump fence taken in the late 1800s. When land was cleared of trees for farming, pine stumps were drawn to a field's edge to make a fence. Any openings that cattle or horses might get through were closed by laying a rail between the stumps. Pine stumps lasted many years. There was a stump fence on the Gates farm on Gates Road that lasted until the early 1930s.

had a chance to find the break during daylight hours. It would have been disastrous for a car to hit a cow in the road, both for the cow and the car!

With turkeys, a barbed wire fence is of no use as they would walk under it or fly over it. In addition, when growing turkeys on pasture, the fence is important to help keep predators out of the pasture and to prevent them from enjoying an early Thanksgiving dinner. As a result, each spring we built a five foot high woven wire fence around our turkey pastures. Because of the winter snows the fence had to be taken down each year. This prevented it from being ruined by the heavy winter snow.

The fence for the turkeys had to be tight to prevent foxes, raccoons and stray dogs from going underneath. We built a special fence stretcher and attached it to the fence every 10 rods, pulling the fence "violin string tight" to deter those predators. Whenever we crossed a slight depression we used an additional post to hold the fence tightly to the ground.

Since the turkey fence needed to be built each spring and taken down in the fall, we used iron stakes with hooks to easily fasten the fence to the posts and hold the fence erect. This type of post made it easy to dismantle the fence in the fall. We often built our turkey fences in June or July when the ground was quite dry. This made driving the posts difficult and was a good way to determine a man's stamina. The driver was a heavy pipe with a weight on top that fitted over the post. Two men held the driver with both hands and forced it up and down Sometimes the post would hit a stone and we would have to start over. At other times it might take two men as many as 50 strokes to drive the post to the proper depth

During the 1930s and 40s domestic turkeys were still quite similar to the wild turkey and could easily fly over the fence. Feed and water were always available inside the fence so no sooner than they had gotten out, they wanted to get back in. They never had enough sense to fly back inside the fence. This required us to check the field periodically during the day and again just before dark to drive them back inside the fence.

Changes in agricultural methods have almost eliminated the annual chore of building and repairing fences. Some dairy and horse farms still pasture their cattle but generally use easily installed and movable electric fences. Most of the wet and hilly land that was one time cleared of trees and stumps for permanent pasture has now reverted back to forest.

Market

The Syracuse Public Market was important to our farm for many years. Although we had to travel 20 miles to reach the market, there were few alternatives for direct marketing to the consumer. I have no record of when we first sold potatoes at the market but my mother indicated that we sold potatoes there in 1900, when she was a little girl. I remember distinctly that 1972 was the last year we sold turkeys on the market, because our turkeys became more readily available when we opened Plainville Farms Restaurant & Store at Cicero.

My mother often told of being at the Syracuse Market with potatoes on November 11,1918 at 11:00 a.m. when the Armistice ending World War I was signed. She said they had a difficult time restraining their horses because of noise from church bells, automobile horns and fire crackers celebrating the end of the war. Five years later, it was the potatoes we took to the market that started turkey growing on our farm. That is a story for another chapter, however.

Each fall, until the 1950s when we discontinued growing potatoes, most of our potatoes were sold at the market. A few days before Thanksgiving, Christmas, New Years and sometimes Saturdays into January and February we took dressed turkeys to the market for sale. The Syracuse Farmers' Market was located at North Salina and Pearl Streets from 1899 to 1938. In 1938 it moved to the Central New York Regional Market, located on Park St. at the northern edge of Syracuse. I remember attending the downtown market with my dad but most of my experiences were at the Regional Market.

Quite often Dad had some live turkeys left after New Year's Day. Since we had no freezer facilities on the farm, he had to feed them until they were sold. He dressed about 20 turkeys a week and took them to the Syracuse Regional Market each Saturday morning until all of the turkeys had been slaughtered. In 1946, we had a terrible snowstorm and our road was impassable for a week. The snow settled during the week, especially where horses and bobs had been traveling over the snow on the highway. The snow didn't deter my dad. He dressed the usual 20 turkeys, loaded them on his small truck and hooked a team of horses to the front of the truck. I still vividly remember the horses pulling the truck, on top of the snow banks, about 1,500 feet to where the road had been plowed. He then drove to market and sold his turkeys.

Selling products on the market was an excellent learning experience for a boy. There were customers who had come from many countries, speaking a variety of languages, owners of dozens of small independent markets and a large number of hucksters who peddled their fruit and vegetables from door to door throughout the city and larger suburban villages. Some were hard to understand and others tried to squeeze every penny they could before making a purchase.

Our presence with dressed turkeys, on the market year after year, gradually built a loyal following of customers. Grocery stores and meat markets sometimes needed to fill a late customer order and would buy a turkey from us. After learning from the customer how good the turkey was, they often ordered all of their turkeys from us for the next Thanksgiving or Christmas holiday. Gradually demand grew for our turkeys.

During World War II and as long as we continued to take turkeys to the market, the market manager arranged to meet us at 4:00 a.m. to weigh the turkeys before the market opened. It was required that all meat and poultry be weighed on the market's scales to assure that the customers received what they were paying for. With customers lining up to buy turkeys there would have been mass confusion if we had to take one turkey at a time to the scale to be weighed. Two very fine gentlemen that provided this service for many years were Charlie Doehner and Gerald Hurley. Usually the turkeys were weighed by 5:00 a.m. and we would go to the small restaurant at the market and have some breakfast.

If there was time we went upstairs to the radio studio of Deacon Doubleday who was an icon in farm broadcasting for many years.

During the winter the market opened at 6:00 a.m. Farmers and dealers were allowed to set up their produce in their stall but could not sell anything until the lights came on and the public was allowed to come into the sheds where the farmers were set up. There was a great deal of activity during the first hour as storekeepers and hucksters quickly filled their needs and then continued on with their day's work. The general public, except for some early risers, arrived later and were less hurried in their purchases. Since the market closed at 2:00 p.m., there were always a few buyers who came late, looking for bargains from a farmer who had unsold merchandise.

The 1930s and 40s was a period when many market customers chose to buy live poultry to prepare for eating at home. There were also others who simply wanted to know that their poultry was freshly killed. To satisfy the desires of the latter, a poultry dressing operation was set up on the market. People could take their chicken, duck or turkey to this dressing plant where it would be prepared for cooking while they waited. It was fascinating to see a wide variety of poultry being dressed for the end users. We chose not to take live turkeys to the market because we preferred to have our brand identification, which would be lost by selling live birds.

The reason we chose to discontinue selling on the market was that Syracuse area customers could buy their fresh Plainville turkeys conveniently at our Cicero store and it eliminated the added work of sending a truck and people to the market. It was a wise decision as turkey sales at our Cicero store the first year were double what they would have been at the market. We appreciated the direct marketing opportunity to the consumer that was made available by the market and today many small farms are continuing to use public markets to help build their businesses.

Farmers' Lung

A great deal had been said and written about 'Coal Miners' Lung', a serious illness resulting from breathing dust in coal mines. A common disease of farmers, which went unrecognized for many years, was 'farmers' lung'. It went unnoticed either because the farmer died before reaching old age or it was just considered a side-effect of getting old.

The farmer breathed dust when he performed many of the necessary farm tasks. There were no protective masks available, until recent years, to filter the dust out of the air you breathe. Dust was just part of most jobs and largely ignored. The only time I remember anyone trying to remove some dust from the air being breathed was when my dad was building a large straw stack in the barnyard when wheat was being threshed. At those times, he tied a large red handkerchief over his nose, giving him the appearance of a train robber.

Dust was almost everywhere on the farm. Loose hair, dust and dirt had to be regularly cleaned from the coats of horses and cows with a curry comb. Hay, which was usually very dusty because farmers cut it when it was about ripe, had to be pitched from the mow and then pitched again when it was fed to the animals. On a nice day, sunlight shining through cracks in the side of the barn illuminated thousands of fine particles of dust floating in the air.

Every job involved in threshing oats and wheat in the barn released large quantities of dust. Removing the kernels from ears of corn sent dust flying into the air. Potatoes, coming out of the ground and stored in the potato cellar emitted large quantities of dust as they were graded and packaged.

We often consider the air we breathe in the open to be clean. Many times it is clean unless the farmer is preparing a seedbed or planting a crop when the ground is dry. In dry conditions large quantities of dust enter the farmers' lungs when driving horses or a tractor without a cab.

Probably much of the dust I breathed came from the turkeys. For each flock of turkeys, a bed of dried shredded sugarcane was spread on the floor of the building to catch their droppings and keep the floor dry. The sugarcane, appropriately named Staz-Dry, was full of dust leaving my exterior a dirty brown after I opened the bales and tore them apart. Quite likely my lungs were filled with some of the same dust. Heat in the buildings, to keep the turkeys warm, made it even dustier when we cleaned the buildings after the turkeys had been removed. Often, after heavy exposure to dust for a day, I would ache in every bone afterwards, an effect not uncommon among many farmers.

When I was about 40 years old, I had a serious health issue with dust. The amount of dust necessary to affect a person is partially genetic. My grandfather had asthma and my mother, although she wasn't in much farm dust, was seriously affected by dust. This genetic trait was passed on to me, and although I was able to tolerate dust eventually my nose stopped functioning. Regardless of my wishes, I had to remove myself from as much of the dust as I could. Devices to wear over a person's nose became available and we put those into use. I delegated more of the work with the crops and turkeys to others while spending more of my time with processing and marketing where there was a limited amount of dust. Eventually my nose started working again and I was able to be in moderate amounts of dust. In retrospect, my problem with dust was a wake-up call that prevented me from developing farmers' lung later in life.

Years ago, a young man growing up on a farm had no choice but to make his vocation farming, as that was what he was expected to do. I am sure some men had difficult lives because of dust poisoning their system. My grandson, Asher, is very allergic to dust from horses and possibly many other kinds of dust. When I had a team of driving horses and a riding horse, he enjoyed them but, almost as quickly as he got near them, he was unable to breathe. Farming, in years past, would not have been a wise career choice for a young man like him.

Farming can be a dangerous occupation in many ways, however, for many years dust usually has been overlooked as a hazard. Dust stealthily steals the breathe from a farmer's lungs. Fortunately today, most farm tractors and combines have filtered air entering the cabs and there is much less exposure to dust. There are also effective breathing masks that a person can easily slip on when working in a dusty area. There can be a tendency to ignore this safety equipment but it is as important as strapping on a parachute when jumping from an airplane, a bit slower perhaps but almost as deadly.

Picking Stone

After picking stones from the same field for several years, many farm boys have wondered who comes stealthily during the night and replaces the stones that were removed. Like magic, the field is picked free of stones one year and in the following year, there they are again, just as many are waiting to be picked up.

When my ancestors first farmed our land, over 175 years ago, they picked stone from the fields, a job that still continues. When the glaciers came down from Canada, thousands of years ago, our US Immigration officers must have been distracted to allow all of those stones to come across the border!

On our farm there are 20 to 40 feet of glacial till, above the bed rock, with stones of all sizes scattered throughout. Freezing and thawing during the wintertime has a lifting effect upon stones lying near the surface, gradually bringing them up. Also, over the years, there has been erosion that washed away the smaller particles of earth and left the stones. As little as one-sixteenth of an inch of soil erosion each year amounts to over six inches in a century.

Originally, many of the first stones picked up from the fields were used for stone fences. When not used for fences they were put into piles, conveniently scattered around the fields, so they wouldn't have to be moved very far. Often, the beginning of a stone pile was a huge stone, too large to be moved.

Few farmers ignored the large stones and left them resting with a huge family of smaller ones surrounding them. In most cases, when the top of a large stone was visible, the farmer went to work with shovel and bar, digging until a chain could be fastened around it. A yoke of oxen, a team of horses and later a tractor pulled it out of the ground onto a stone boat and then dragged it away. I have had this experience many times.

If the stone was too large to move, there were two possibilities for the farmer that insisted on stone free fields. One way was the use of dynamite to break the stone into smaller pieces and the other was to bury it. When burying a stone, a hole had to be dug on one side at least three feet deeper than the bottom of the stone. This sometimes was deeper than the man was tall. Homer Abbott told me of doing this when he was a young man on the Abbott Homestead. I specifically remember a man near Liverpool being crushed to death when a stone he was burying fell on him.

In the early 1900s, extending into the 1930s, a good use was found for the stones that farmers had accumulated in stone piles and stone fences. Improved roads were needed for the newly invented automobile and crushed stone was excellent for both a road base and mixing with sand and cement to form a hard, durable road surface. Many farmers in Central NY loaded their stones on a wagon, pulled by a team of horses and hauled the stones to a steam powered stone crusher used in building roads. My dad earned extra money doing this about 1921.

My dad and I bought a number of farms over the years with old stone fences and stone piles that for some reason never made it to a road base via the stone crusher. Our solution, to make these stones disappear, was quite simple. We used a bulldozer to dig a huge hole and then push all of the stones into it and cover them with dirt.

Until the later 1800s, hay, oats and wheat were cut by a man swinging a scythe or grain cradle. The long sharp blades skimmed close to the ground as the stalks were cut. If the blade hit a stone, the blade would be dulled or even bent. It would waste time to stop to straighten and sharpen the blade. Because of this, a good farmer always was careful to remove stones, even down to two inches in diameter, from the surface of the ground.

By the time I arrived on earth, mowing machines and grain binders had come into use and it was not necessary to remove stones as small as in the past. I believe it was difficult for my dad not to pick up the smaller stones because he had me use a five-tinged fork to pick them up. Something similar happened to me as I got older. It was hard for me to leave stones larger than I had picked up in the past. Once something is ingrained in a person, changing can be difficult, even if the change requires less effort.

For generations, farm children have been required to help pick stone at an early age. It's fun for only a few minutes and then questions, asked by farm children for generations begin; "When are we gonna be done?" "Can I go home now?" or simply, "I'm tired." The presence of stones will continue for generations but as farm operations increase in size and mechanization advances, the farm child of today sits in an air conditioned cab, driving a tractor that is pulling a mechanical stone picker.

Ditching

The glaciers passing over Central New York thousands of years ago, left more than rocks and fertile soil. The landscape that remained is punctuated with large hills and valleys as well as much smaller changes of elevation within almost any farm field. Because of this there are pockets of various sizes in many farm fields that hold water and prevent proper drainage.

Initially, when the land was cleared, farmers tilled land around huge tree stumps and avoided the wet depressions. As tree stumps were gradually removed and farmers were able to farm an increased amount of land, it was more efficient to till rectangular fields without having to circumvent wet areas. A shovel and a plow could be used to make an open ditch for draining a shallow area but once an open ditch was made it was necessary to continually work around the ditch.

Several simple methods were devised to drain water underground. One was to dig a ditch about three feet deep and lay about a foot of small tree branches in the bottom, cover them with about a foot of old hay, straw or weeds to keep the dirt from entering the spaces between the branches and then cover it over with dirt. This type of underground drain was inexpensive and simple to construct. One time I was involved in an archeological dig for Native American relics and the archeologist thought an old underground ditch was the remnants of an Indian village until I explained to him that it was a type of drainage used by early settlers.

Another method of underground drainage was to dig a similar ditch and fill the bottom foot with field stone not larger than half the width of the ditch. These stones were covered with hay or straw and then topped with dirt. A ditch made in this manner was not capable of carrying a large flow of water but lasted for many years. A superior adaptation of this method was to lay two parallel rows of stones in the bottom of the ditch and cap them with flat stones, leaving an open trench down the middle. These stones were covered with hay or straw and then dirt was put on top. A ditch made in this manner functioned well for more than a hundred years when properly cared for.

John Johnston came to the Geneva area from Scotland and installed the first clay drain tile in New York, which were shipped from Scotland, on his farm at Geneva in 1835. The results were remarkable and clay drain tile began to be produced in scattered locations through the northeast. Many miles of clay tile, each a foot long, were made in nearby Warners.

Miles and miles of underground drains were dug by hand with shovel and pick until about 1940. Sometimes an ordinary horse drawn plow was used to cut through the top foot of earth but the rest was dug by hand. Every so often a large stone was encountered that had to be moved. I was fortunate to have been born about the time mechanical ditchers came into use. I remember my father obtained two unemployed men in 1941 and put them to work digging a ditch 1000 feet long by hand. Fortunately my ditch digging by hand involved shorter distances.

I helped install several miles of clay tile drains on our farm. In the process we cut across a great variety of underground drains including many stone ditches that I repaired as we crossed them. We also found a wide variety of clay tile. Some were shaped similar to a horse shoe, some with a board underneath and even drains made of two boards nailed together to form an inverted V. Some drains were working and others were not. It is essential that the underground drain be installed properly and the outlet kept continually open. As farms changed hands, drains were forgotten and became of no use.

Bill McLennan ran the tile factory in Warners until it closed and then purchased a ditching machine to install tile ditches for farmers. He hired a helper and the farmer furnished two helpers. He usually spent about a week each year putting in ditches on our farm. Bill ran a string line, fastened to stakes along the path of the proposed ditch at the proper grade

A view of a few of the great variety of clay tile, used to drain farm land, on display at a tile museum near Geneva.

for the tile being installed at the bottom of the ditch. As we laid and covered the tile we made sure that a stone didn't damage a tile.

Ditching was hard work, especially on a hot summer day. I always enjoyed working with Bill, however, because he did the work well and didn't waste any time. Bill wasn't building a cathedral, only a tile ditch but Bill took pride in doing things right.

With the invention of plastic tile in about 1970, the work of laying tile became easier because the plastic tile came in long rolls, of various diameters. It simplified handling and was not subject to breakage as easily as clay tile. Today, installing underground drainage is even more simplified with the use of lasers to determine grade, and huge tractors that make an opening and install the tile with hardly disturbing the top of the ground. Under good conditions, several miles of tile can be installed in a day with one of these machines compared to perhaps 100 feet by one man when the ditch was dug and covered by hand.

Wells and Water Witching

I am the type of person that likes to be able to understand 'cause and effect,' but when it comes to water witching I understand nothing. I have seen water witching many times and with some people it is unbelievably accurate.

A turkey farm with a processing plant requires great quantities of water. On our farm, the soils and the rock underneath offered opportunities for many wells but none of great abundance. As our business continually grew, for 20 years we were almost constantly digging or drilling new wells. With at least three wells we ran into salt that made the water unacceptable.

Maynard Hencle was a good friend who had the extraordinary gift of locating underground streams of water. Several times I asked him to help us locate water. He would go to a fruit tree, take his jackknife and cut a small crotch and we would start walking near where we needed the water. If there was a point where two veins crossed we would pick that spot with the hope of obtaining a larger supply with two veins. If he estimated the depth of each vein was within the reach of a backhoe, we dug the well. Amazingly we would find small gravel veins of water at the depth and location he indicated.

One time, Maynard located a strong vein of water about 80 feet deep and we followed it more than 1,000 feet to a point where it came within 15 feet of ground level. It was on one edge of a narrow valley a few feet up the hillside. I questioned his location because I anticipated the vein would follow the path of least resistance and be in the bottom of the valley. We brought in a large backhoe, dug down 15 feet at the spot he designated and found a nice gravel vein of water. Not to be deterred,

I ordered the backhoe operator to dig across the width of the valley to obtain even more water and we didn't gain an extra drop!

A few years later, as we were increasingly used more water, my neighbor Pat Voorhees gave me permission to look for water on his farm adjacent to the Seneca River. I hired a geologist to do a study and locate the general area. Then I asked Maynard to identify an exact spot. We drilled a well at that spot with tremendous success. It provided a large quantity of good water.

The well was a mile away and about 100 feet lower than the processing plant on our farm. I envisioned running an inch and a half or a two inch pipe but fortunately Cliff Lamb gave me some good advice. He said, "Bob, run a four inch line and build a reservoir by the processing plant to hold more than a day's water needs." I followed his advice with the four inch line and constructed a 60,000 gallon underground reservoir near the processing plant. Later, there were many times I appreciated Cliff's wise advice. As water usage continued to increase we added two more wells and pumps in the same area and the pipe was able to handle the water from them all.

To install the pipe, which came in 20 foot lengths with neoprene joints, I hired my ditch digging friend Bill McLennan. We were given permission by the local municipality to run the water line in the highway right of way. Because of this, we buried the pipe five feet deep so it would never be in the way and so it was below the frost line. My men, Mark and I installed the pipe, which was a major undertaking. We made certain that the pipe was bedded in sand and installed concrete bulkheads wherever the pipe took a turn. One area we ran the pipe through was full of poison ivy. The juice from its roots gave all of us who were working in the trench, a good case of poison ivy. Amazingly, we installed this pipe 40 years ago and have never had even a minor problem.

Because we continued to add outlying farms for growing turkeys it was usually necessary to locate an adequate supply of water on each farm. When we were building turkey buildings on the Stachurski farm

I had one of our team members use a backhoe to dig for water, but without success. Maynard was quite old at the time but came one cold November morning with a crotch stick and started walking around where we were planning to have the turkey buildings. It was difficult for him to walk very far and I was afraid he had lost his touch. He said, "Bob, dig anyplace in this general area." The area he pointed out covered several acres so now I was almost certain he had lost his touch.

I followed his advice, however, and at only nine feet, the level where he said it would be, we found all the water we needed to grow over 100,000 turkeys a year! No, I don't understand how he did it. In my hands the crotch stick didn't move unless I physically made it move. In Maynard's hands, he didn't have enough strength to keep it from moving when he stood over a good vein of water.

Turkeys

Turkeys were a part of our farm, which was one of the first farms to grow more than 100 turkeys and dress them for market. We grew several thousand turkeys and purchased additional live turkeys from farmers in Northern New York.

Turkeys came to Plainville through a stroke of fate. Dad and Grandfather regularly sold their potatoes at the Syracuse Public Farmer's market. In November 1923, a small turkey grower from Northern New York had eight live turkeys that he had been unable to sell at the market, the market was closing, and he did not want to take them home. My dad bought them and brought them to our farm at Plainville to fatten them up and take back to the market, along with his potatoes, for sale at Christmas time.

Apparently Dad and Grandfather enjoyed their decision to purchase the turkeys because the next year a small flock of turkeys became part of the farm's operation. Within a decade several thousand were being grown and our farm was one of the earliest to become involved in what was, at that time, considered to be a commercial turkey operation. My dad and grandfather never regarded turkeys to be more than just a part of their farm operation.

From March through June a flock of breeders was kept and every two weeks eggs were taken to a hatchery near Watertown and later a hatchery in Skaneateles. Four weeks later the hatched poults were picked up at the hatchery and started life in small 12 x 14 foot brooder houses. The brooder houses each had an oil stove for heat and a wire floor sunporch on the south side of the brooder house to permit the poults to be outside in good weather.

Sign at Plainville Turkey Farm from 1930 to 1952. The barn on the left held 11 dairy cows and the one next to it held dairy heifers, horses, potatoes, hay and bundles of grain prior to threshing.

At eight weeks of age the poults were caught, put into crates and taken to a fenced in pasture where they stayed until they were ready to be marketed. Because of disease and a variety of animals of prey we were fortunate if we could market 75% of the poults we started.

We built a fence around the turkey pasture and had a man with a shotgun and a dog stay with the turkeys at night but it was impossible to completely eliminate predators. Owls and hawks flew into the field, foxes dug under the fence and a few human beings felt that the turkeys were there for the taking.

Twice a day feed, consisting of a mash, wheat, oats and corn, along with water, was hauled to the turkeys with horse and wagon. Skim milk was purchased from area creameries to pour on top of their mash. Turkey nutrition was in its infancy but the combination of feeds, skim milk and pasture combined to produce good turkeys.

A special catching cage was put together because domestic turkeys could fly as well as wild turkeys. They were put into large crates, made

Turkey breeder hens. The large barn had been constructed as a tobacco shed. The breeder hens used the portion on the right. The area behind the windows was the turkey processing area.

from used tobacco boxes and taken to the tobacco stripping room to be processed. The tobacco stripping room was very crude and had no running water or refrigeration. The turkeys were bled and their feathers removed, which was referred to as New York dressed. The stores and restaurants that purchased the turkeys completed the dressing process. By not cutting the turkey, other than for bleeding, the turkey had a much longer shelf life without refrigeration.

In 1949, a letter came from the NYS Department of Agriculture and Markets saying, improve your turkey processing facilities or we will shut you down. A decision had to be made to get in or get out of turkeys and we decided to stay in. A small processing plant was constructed the next year and turkeys continued to be a part of the farm's operation.

Few people enjoyed turkey in the 1930s as they were expensive to grow and even though they sold for only 30 or 40 cents a pound the cost of a turkey represented a week's wages for many people. Christmas was the largest market for turkeys with Thanksgiving coming in second. A few turkeys were sold almost every month. The flocks produced for meat

White and bronze turkeys on pasture. The small building is where the man guarding the turkeys slept at night with his shotgun and dog nearby. In the back of the photo is a high pole that had a trap on top to catch owls looking for a turkey dinner.

Bob Bitz, Gates Hudson and Arthur Hudson moving New York dressed turkeys, on a pair of bobs pulled by horses, to the cellar of the house for overnight storage to keep the turkeys from freezing. Circa 1937

were sold from October through March and during the next several months the breeding flock was gradually sold. Turkey eggs were part of our household diet because we ate any eggs produced before saving them for hatching. We also ate cracked eggs, small eggs and the occasional double-yolked eggs.

During the 60 years following 1950 there were many changes in the turkey growing operation at Plainville Turkey Farm but that is part of another story.